FOR YOUNG BEGINNERS
CHESS

The position of the men at the start. White has made his first move. Each Queen starts the game on a square of her own colour – the White Queen on a white square, the Black Queen on a black square.

FOR YOUNG BEGINNERS
CHESS

♛ by William T. McLeod and Ronald Mongredien ♚

illustrated by Jean-Paul Colbus

GOLDEN PRESS • NEW YORK

Western Publishing Company, Inc.
Racine, Wisconsin

© text 1975 W.T. McLeod and R. Mongredien
© illustrations 1975 Editions des deux Coqs D'Or, Paris
U.S. edition published 1977 by Golden Press, New York.
Western Publishing Company, Inc.
Printed in U.S.A.

All rights reserved. No part of this book may be reproduced or copied
in any form without written permission from the publisher.

Golden, a Golden Book® and Golden Press® are trademarks
of Western Publishing Company, Inc.

Library of Congress Catalog Card Number: 76-49743

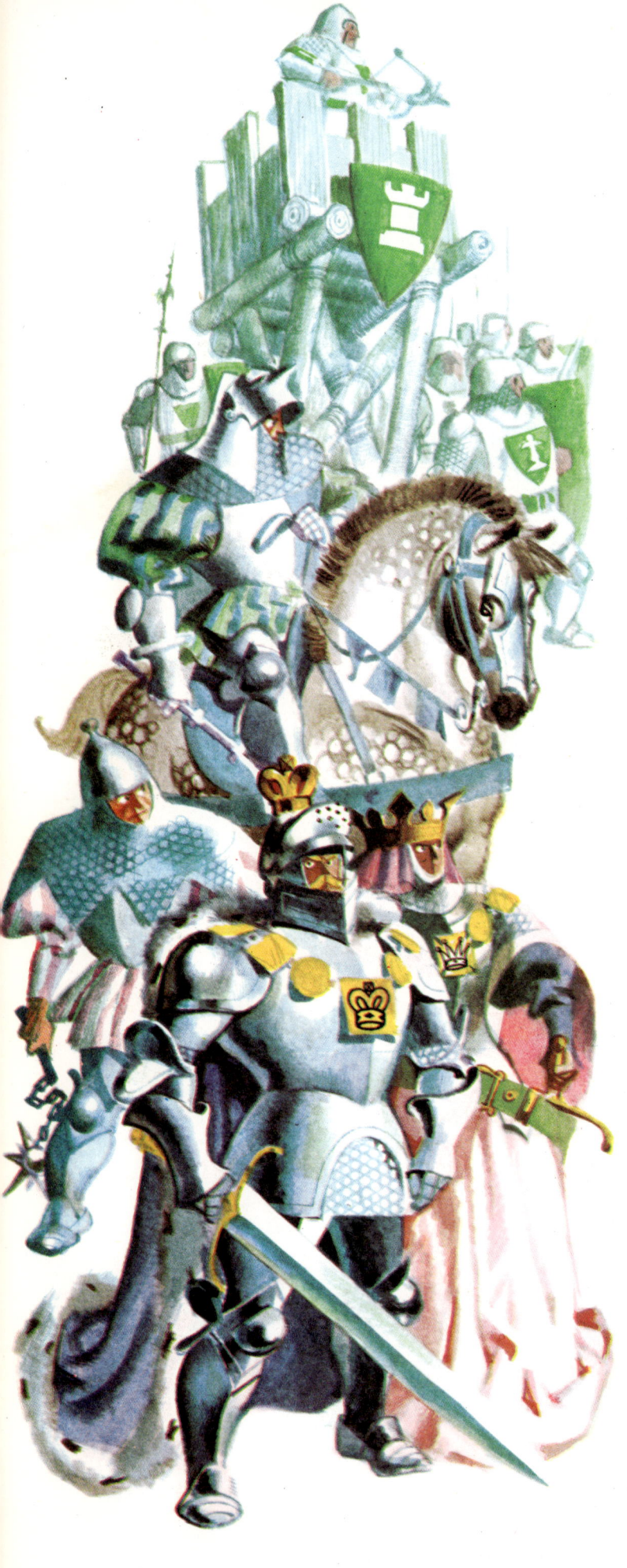

Contents

The Armies	8
The Battlefield	10
Pawns	10
The Knight	16
The Bishop	20
The Rook	23
The Queen	26
The King	28
Check	29
Checkmate	30
Attack	34
Defence	36
Castling	38
A King's Side Game	39
How to Start	40
Tactics	44
Pins	45
Forks	46
Exchanging	48
Discovered Attack	50
Sacrifice	51
How to Finish	52
Useful Hints	55
Notation	56
Drawn Games	57
Words You Should Know	58
Answers	59

About this Book

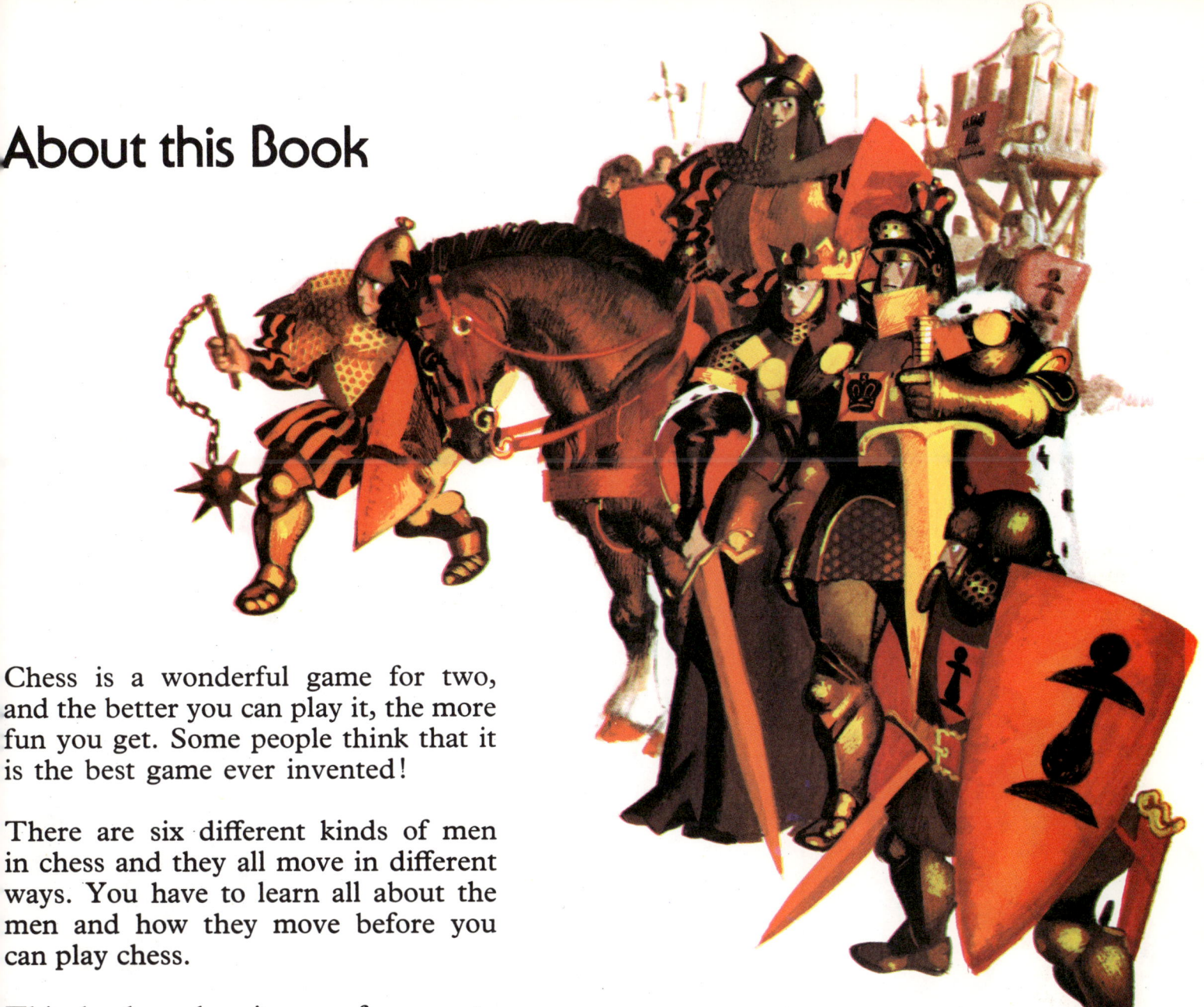

Chess is a wonderful game for two, and the better you can play it, the more fun you get. Some people think that it is the best game ever invented!

There are six different kinds of men in chess and they all move in different ways. You have to learn all about the men and how they move before you can play chess.

This book makes it easy for you to learn how to play. It talks about each kind of man one at a time and gives you plenty of interesting games to play while you are learning.

If you read slowly, and if you really do play all the learning games with a friend, we promise that both of you will be playing real chess and getting real fun out of it by the time you have finished the book.

It is important to read this book with a friend who wants to learn chess, too. Play all the games you are told about with him or her. This is the best way to learn. Always have your chess board and men beside you when you are reading the book, and set up on your own board the positions shown in the pictures.

The Authors

The Chessmen

Chess is a game of war between two armies, called WHITE and BLACK.

You are the General commanding one army, and the person you are playing against leads the other army.

Each army tries to capture the enemy King. If a King is captured, that army has lost the war, and the game is over.

Like all armies, your chess army has different kinds of soldiers in it. You can see them in the pictures below.

Here is the chess army you must learn to lead

8 foot-soldiers. They are called PAWNS.

2 cavalry officers. They are called KNIGHTS.

2 company commanders. They are called BISHOPS.

They depend on you for victory

2 battalion commanders. They are called ROOKS.

1 army commander. This is the QUEEN — an unusual army with a lady in command, but she is a very important person, as you will see later on.

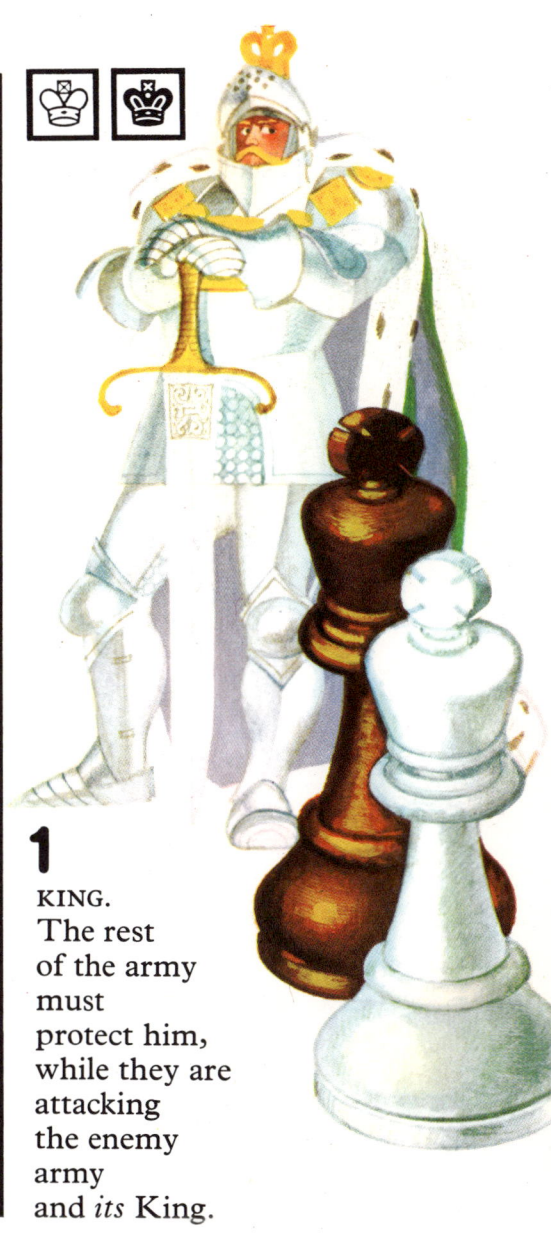

1 KING. The rest of the army must protect him, while they are attacking the enemy army and *its* King.

9

The Battlefield

The battle takes place on the CHESSBOARD, shown in the picture.

You can see that it has squares, coloured light and dark. We say "White" and "Black" even if the squares on your board are white and red, or any other two colours.

There are eight rows of squares and each row has eight squares in it. How many squares does this make?

The board is *always* placed so that each player has a white square in his right-hand corner. It is most important to remember this. Notice that *both* armies use all the squares on the board, black *and* white squares.

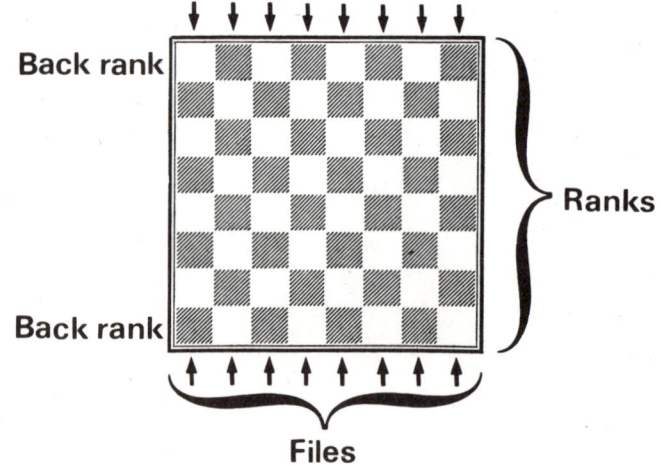

We can now name the rows as shown in the diagram. Each row *across* the board is called a RANK. There are eight ranks.

Each row up and down the board is called a FILE. (Think of "single file".) How many files are there?

Now we are ready to meet your army, and we begin with the foot-soldiers.

Pawns

Pawns are the foot-soldiers. The name comes from the Latin word meaning "foot" and means "the walkers".

As in real armies, there are more of them than of any other kind of soldier. How many Pawns do you have in your army? (Look back at page 8, if you have forgotten.)

Black plays Here

You must have a WHITE square here.

White plays Here

How the Pawns Move

Pawns move up the board one square at a time. They move slowly, because they go on foot!

But there are two odd things about these foot-soldiers of yours:

1. They can move only forward, never back. They are soldiers that do not know how to run away!

2. The *first* time you move any pawn you can move it *two* squares forward, *but only the first time*. This is so that he can get at the enemy army as soon as possible.

So, remember: you can never move your Pawns back; and the *first* time you move any Pawn you can move it either one square or two squares forward.

For the rest of the game, Pawns move one step (or square) straight ahead.

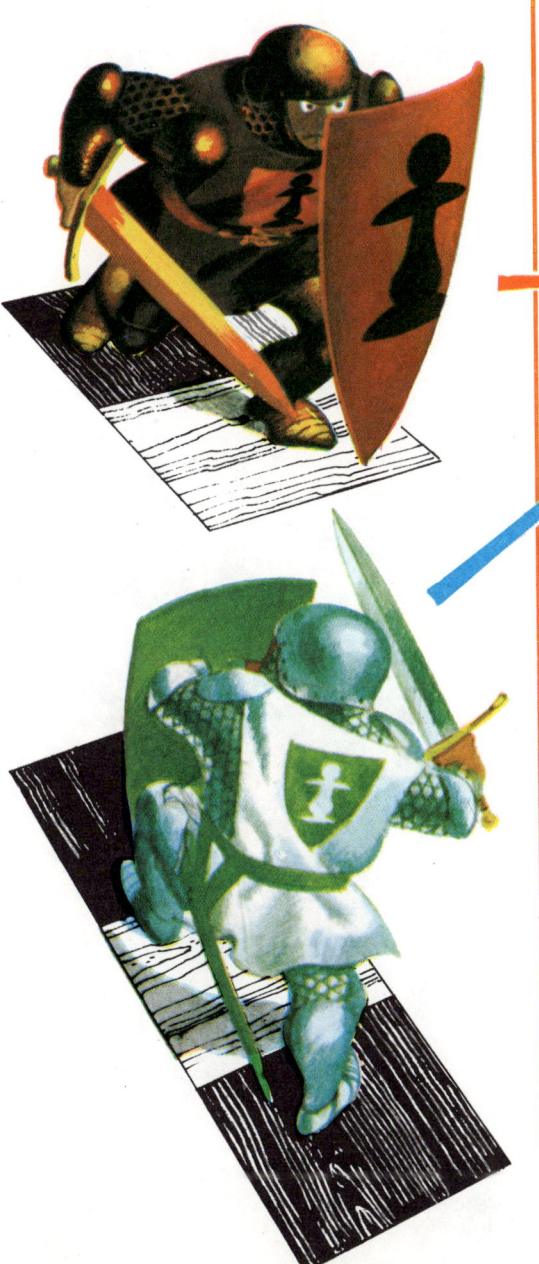

LOOK!

There are lots of pictures like this in the pages that follow. They use the small signs you saw on pages 8 and 9 to show the positions of the men on the board at any point in a game. You must practise reading these pictures, which we call diagrams. Remember: White is *always* playing from the bottom of the board up to the top, and Black from the top to the bottom.

Promotion from the Ranks

There is one other important thing about this foot-soldier. If he can reach the enemy's back rank alive, he is rewarded for his bravery by being promoted to being an officer. His General (you) may make him into any kind of soldier he wishes, but *not* a King. Most generals choose to turn a successful Pawn into the strongest soldier in the army – a Queen. You may do this even if you still have your first Queen on the board.

This is called "queening a Pawn".

How Pawns Capture

Any Pawn can capture any enemy soldier, even the enemy Queen. The Pawn captures in a special way, by moving one square forward at an angle, left or right, on to the file next to its own. Look carefully at the diagram below. The arrows point to the squares that are attacked by the Pawns.

Minefield DANGER!

Look carefully at the diagram below. If you are White, what can you say about the squares marked X?

That's right! They are dangerous! Your soldiers must keep away from them as they would from a minefield. Even your Queen could get blown up on one of these squares! Keep a very sharp lookout for squares like these. Do not move one of your men on to one of these danger squares.

Look at the White Pawns now. Can you put a cross on the minefield squares waiting for your enemy? See answer [*A1*] on page 59.

In the second diagram, Pawns 1 and 2 are both in danger. But there is a difference! If the White Pawn captures, Black loses a Pawn. If the Black Pawn captures, White can *recapture* with Pawn 3 and things are even. Make sure you understand this.

How Pawns get Stuck

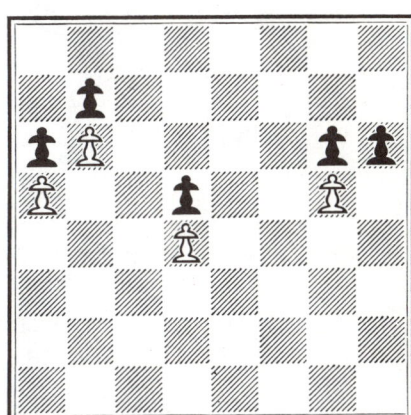

Here you see that when a Pawn meets an enemy soldier head-on, he cannot move at all, forward *or* back. He is stuck, unless he can capture an enemy man on one of the next files. In the diagram above, which pawns are stuck? [*A2*]

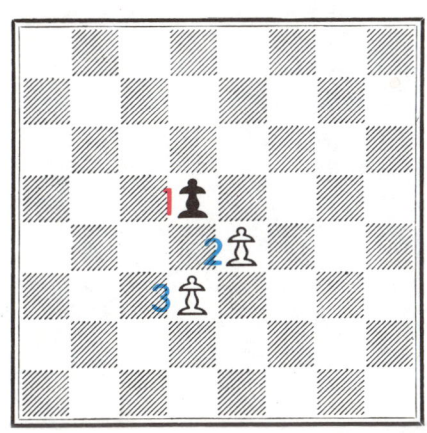

Pawns Help Other Men

Remember that Pawns are good soldiers and support their comrades. They can support officers as well as other foot-soldiers, and they do it very well indeed. Look at the diagrams and see how this works. The Pawn is a gallant fighter against odds.

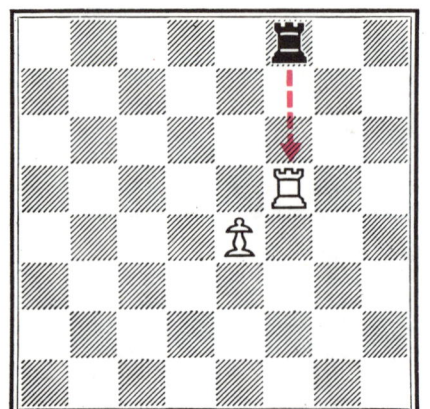

The Black Rook threatens the White Rook: "Death to the White Rook!"

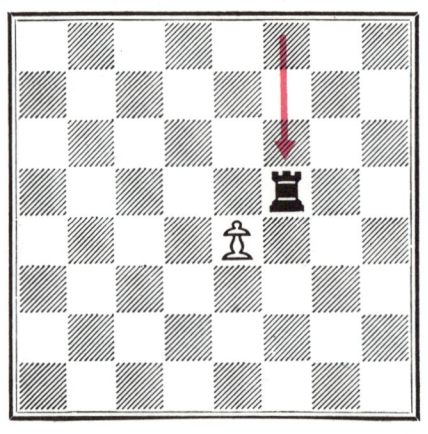

He moves swiftly down the board, crushes the White Rook, and takes his square.

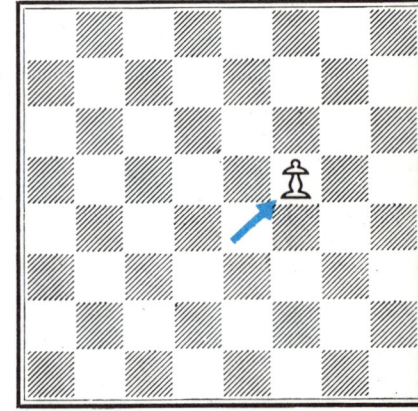

But not for long! The brave little Pawn attacks the monster, who is defeated and sent off the board.

There is one further thing you must remember about capturing – not only about Pawn capturing, but *all* capturing in chess. Even if you *can* capture an enemy man you do not *have* to do so. You can choose whether to capture the enemy at once or leave him in his dangerous minefield and capture him later or not at all. Some soldiers may have to stand in a minefield for a long time!

So, if you have one of your men in a minefield and he is not captured at once, please don't forget about him!

A Pawn Game

CAUTION! Have you got a white square here?

Set up the board with four Pawns for each player, as shown in the picture.

Have you got the white square in the right-hand corner?

Now, remember carefully all you have learned about how the Pawns move and capture (especially that first move!) and see who wins. White always moves first in chess. You take it in turns to move and you *must* move whenever it is your turn.

The winner is the player who gets one of his Pawns to his enemy's back rank first.

Who won? If neither player can get a Pawn through the enemy line to the back rank, the game is a draw.

A sample game to help you is shown below.

Remember to take it in turn to play White. Score one point for a win and half a point for a draw. Who is the winner after twenty pawn games?

Keep on practising this pawn game as long as you want.

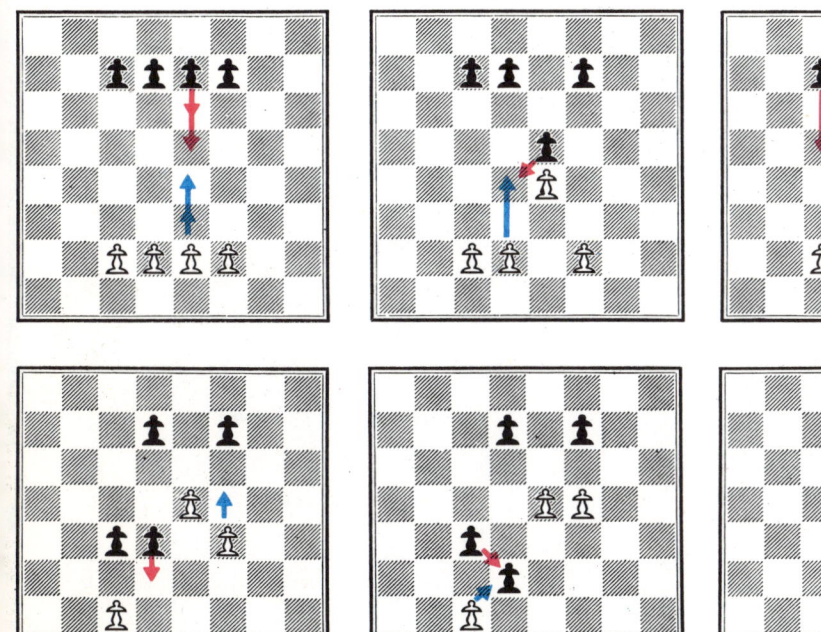

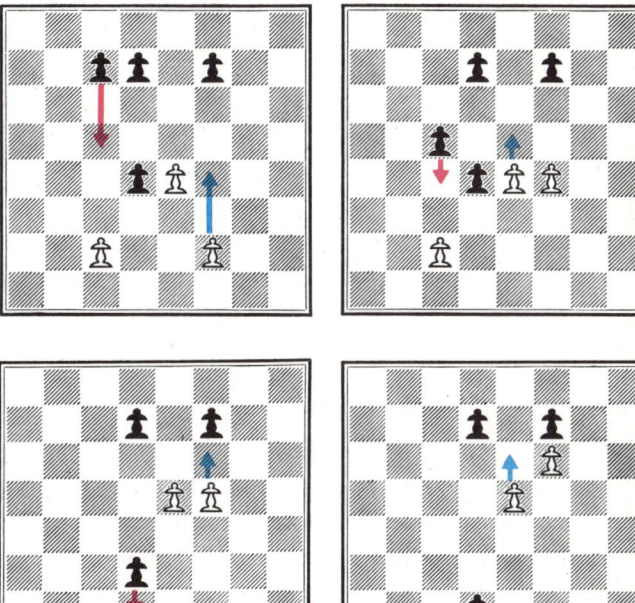

The Knight

From the foot-soldier to the cavalry officer, with his high jumping bold war horse. Yes, this horseman is the *only* piece in the chess army that can jump over another man. He can jump over one of his own army or over an enemy man. For this reason his German name is *Springer* or "Jumper".

More than that, when he moves, in order to avoid the enemy fire, he jumps first one way and then another before he finally lands on his square. Because he can jump about so easily, even on a crowded board, the Knight is usually very busy near the beginning of a game, when the board is crowded with men.

How the Knight Moves

The Knight could be called the two-one piece, because that is exactly how he moves: first two squares forward and then one square either to his left or right.

Unlike the Pawn he *can* move backwards, *and* sideways too. In all he can move in four directions – up the board and back down again, to the right, and to the left. But no matter in which direction he decides to go he always moves two squares, and then one square to either his left *or* right. Look at the diagram.

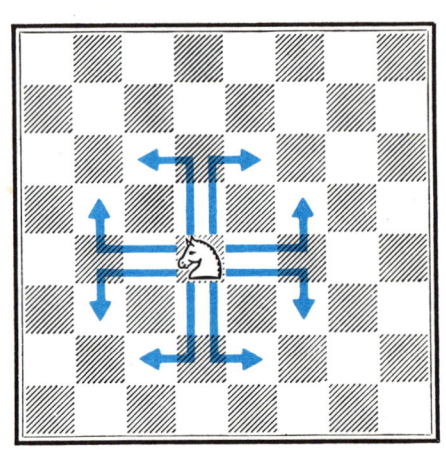

Remember

The Knight's move is shaped like a letter **L**, but the letter can be any way up you choose – upside down, on its back, on its side, and so on.

The Knight always jumps from a light square to a dark square or from a dark square to a light square.

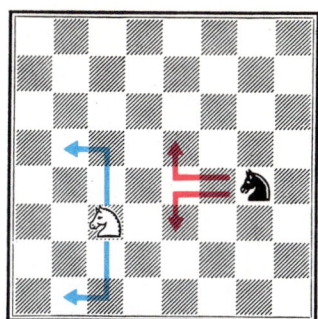

From a light square his sword stretches out to the eight dark squares round him. Any enemy man foolish enough to land on one of these eight squares, unprotected, will soon fall to the Knight's whirling sword.

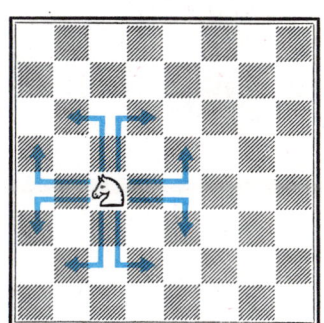

And if the Knight lies in wait on a dark square it is the eight light squares surrounding him which are like dynamite to the enemy.

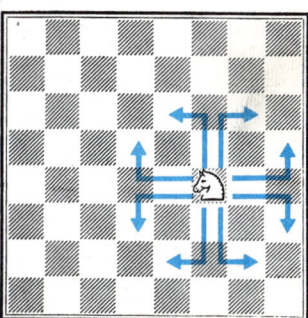

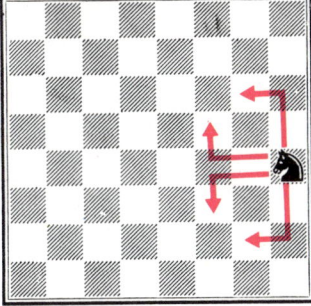

But

See what happens if the Knight moves to the side of the board! Can you say why the Knight in the picture looks so angry? [A3]

How the Knight Captures

Any enemy man standing on a square your Knight can move to may be captured by the Knight. The enemy piece is removed from the board and your Knight moves to that square.

Knight Practice

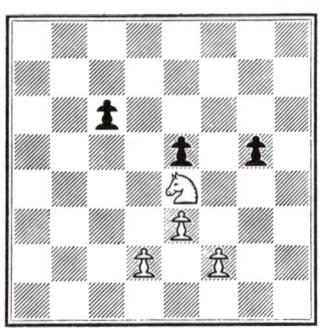

Can the Knight capture? [A4]

Can the Knight capture? [A5]

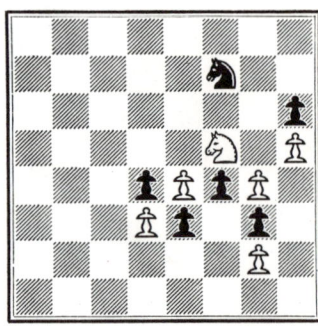

How many men can the White Knight capture without being captured? [A6]

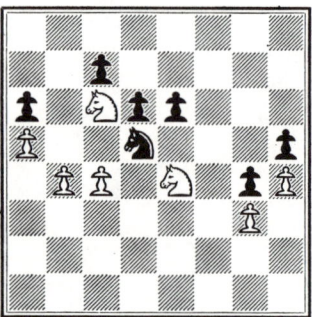

The White Pawn is attacking the Black Knight. Can the Knight escape? [A7]

How many Pawns can the Knight capture if he takes two moves each time? [A8]

In how few moves can the Knight capture the Black Pawn? [A9]

Knight Games

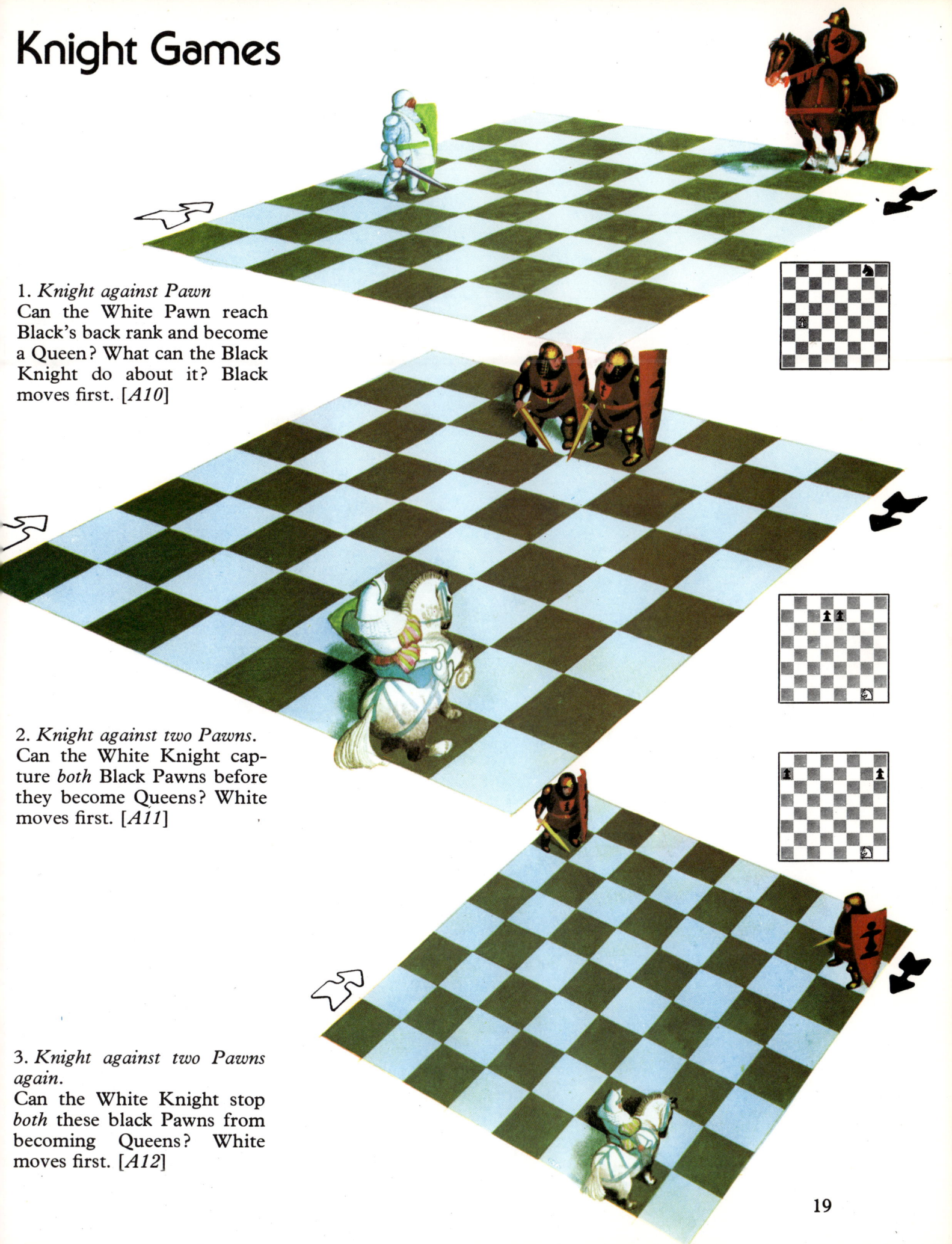

1. Knight against Pawn
Can the White Pawn reach Black's back rank and become a Queen? What can the Black Knight do about it? Black moves first. [A10]

2. Knight against two Pawns.
Can the White Knight capture *both* Black Pawns before they become Queens? White moves first. [A11]

3. Knight against two Pawns again.
Can the White Knight stop *both* these black Pawns from becoming Queens? White moves first. [A12]

19

The Bishop

A Bishop in the army? Actually fighting and capturing the enemy? This will not seem so strange when we remember that in the Middle Ages many Bishops were also powerful princes with armies of their own.

In fact this piece was not always called a Bishop. The Arabs, who brought chess to Spain and gave the game to Europe, called him *al-fil*, "the elephant". In India elephants were used in war to carry soldiers into battle and to break down enemy defences – like the modern tank! Perhaps we should really call the Bishop a tank commander!

How the Bishop Moves

The Bishop moves slantwise up and down the board.

The Bishop can move in four directions – slantwise up the board from left to right and back again; slantwise up the board from right to left and back again.

We say the Bishops move "diagonally" or along a "diagonal" – look at the diagram and make sure you know what a diagonal is.

Notice that one of your Bishops moves on the light squares and one on the dark squares. They never change from light to dark and so they never meet.

When a Bishop meets one of his own men he must stop before he reaches him.

If an enemy man is in his path he must either stop before reaching him or capture the enemy by sending him off the board. He then occupies the square the enemy was on.

The Bishop cannot jump over a man. When another man is in his way he must either stop before he reaches him or capture him by taking over his square. See diagram on right.

Bishop Practice

1. How many squares can the Bishop move to? [*A13*].

2. How many Pawns is the Black Bishop attacking? [*A14*].

3. It is your turn and you can play either White or Black. Which colour would you choose and why? [*A15*]

Bishop Games

1. *How many moves?*
Look at the first picture. How many times must the Bishop move to capture the Pawn? That's right – the Bishop can reach any man (or any square) in two moves. Of course there must not be any pieces in his way!

2. *Bishop against Pawns*
Look at the second picture. Can the Bishop stop both Black Pawns from reaching the back rank and becoming Queens?
   Try it with a friend and see. Take turns at playing the Bishop. White moves first. [*A16*]

Put us down!

3. *Bishop against Pawns again*
Place a White Bishop as shown in the third picture. Now ask Black to place two Pawns anywhere he likes on Black's second rank (the Black Pawns' starting place). Can the Bishop stop either of the Black Pawns from queening?
   Try it and see. [*A17*]

The Rook

The name of this man has nothing to do with birds! It comes (like the game of chess itself) from ancient Persia and India. There the word meant "warrior".

"The Warrior" is a good name, for the Rook is the strongest piece on the board after the Queen. This is why we call him your Battalion Commander, second-in-command to your General, the Queen.

A Rook is sometimes called a castle. This is because the little wall on top of the tower looks like the top of a castle wall.

How the Rook Moves

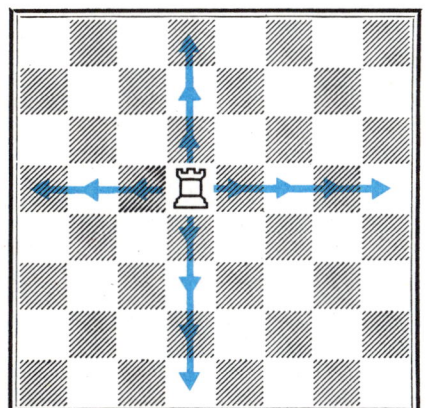

The Rook moves straight up and down or straight across the board.

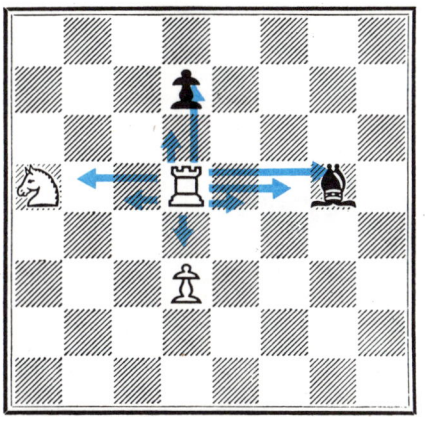

He must either stop before a man in his path or capture him.

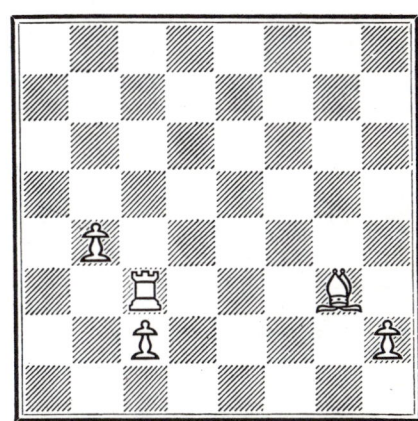

How many squares can the Rook move to? [A18]

The rook can move in four directions — straight up the board and back down again; straight across the board, from right to left and left to right.

The Rook can only move over *empty* squares. This means that when he meets one of his own men he must stop before he reaches him.

If an enemy man is in his path he must either stop before he reaches him or capture the enemy by sending him off the board. He then occupies the square that the enemy was on.

The Rook cannot jump over a man. When another man is in his way he must either stop before he reaches him or capture him by taking over his square.

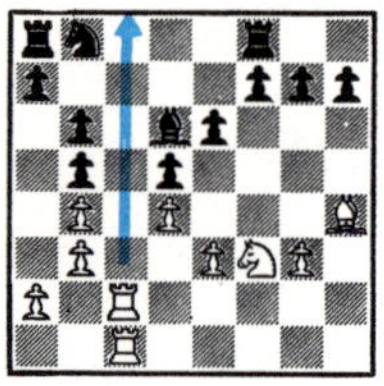

Like senior officers in real armies, the Rook often plans the battle from headquarters (the back rank). From here he supports his troops in the front line and advances only when they have cleared a path for him.

Practice with the Rook

1. How many squares can the Rook move to? [A19]

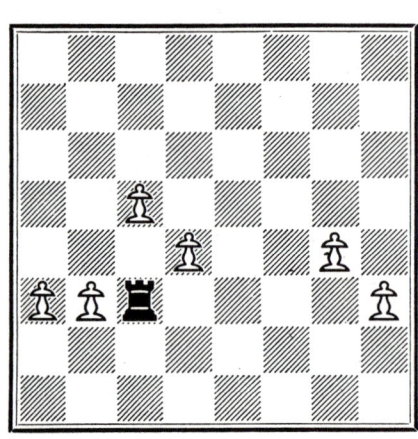

2. How many Pawns is the Black Rook attacking? How many can he capture without being taken? [A20]

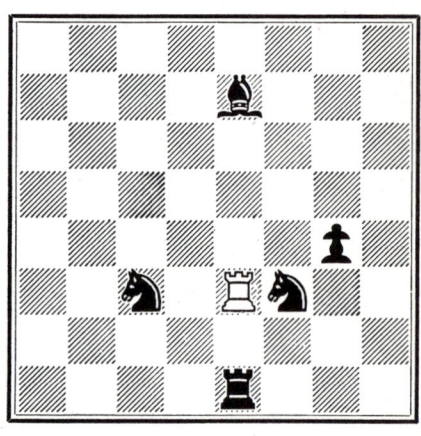

3. What piece can the White Rook capture without being captured himself? [A21]

Rook Games

1. Black to move. Can Black queen one of his Pawns or can the White Rook capture all four? [A23]
   Take turns in playing White.

2. White to move. Can the Black Rook stop the White Pawn from queening, without being captured himself? Take turns in playing White and Black. [A24]

3. Black to move. Here is a chance to find out for yourself which is the stronger piece, the Rook or the Knight. Each player must try to queen his Pawn first or to capture both enemy men.
   Now try the same game again, but put a Black Bishop where the Black Knight was in the first game.
   Have you found out which is the strongest: the Bishop, the Knight, or the Rook? [A25]

4. A fight to a finish. In this game you and your enemy have more men to look after than in any of the games you have played so far. Each player has to try to queen a Pawn first or to capture all the enemy men.
   This is an important game. Play it with your friend *at least* ten times. See who wins most often.

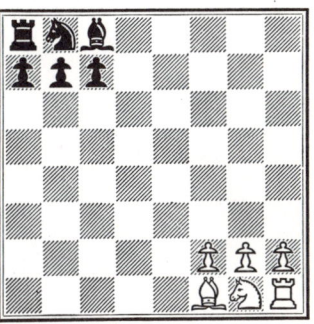

4. It is your turn and you can play either White or Black. Which colour would you choose and why? [A22]

The Queen

The Queen is the strongest piece on the board and the most valuable, after the King. Since she is the General, she stands at the beginning of the battle next to the King, to protect him, and to share with him the planning of the battle.

As she is so valuable she must not join the battle herself too soon, in case she is trapped in an ambush. She must move extra carefully and she usually has a bodyguard.

How the Queen Moves

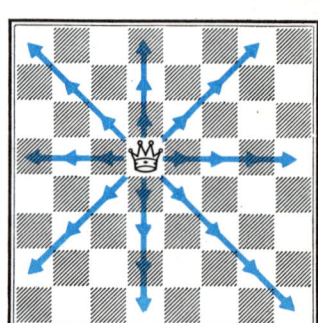

Practice with the Queen

1. How many squares can the Queen move to? [A26]

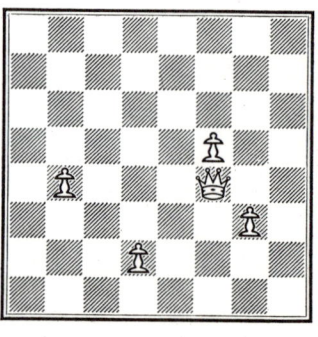

"Watch out for the Queen!"

The Queen can move like a Rook AND like a Bishop. Look at the diagram on the left.

How many directions can the Queen move in? That's right. Eight.

The Queen, like the Bishop and the Rook, may *not* jump over a man. She must either stop before him or (if he is an enemy) capture him.

2. What is the least number of moves the Queen takes to capture the Black Bishop? White to move. [A27]

3. It is your turn and you can choose which colour to play. Would you choose White or Black? [A28]

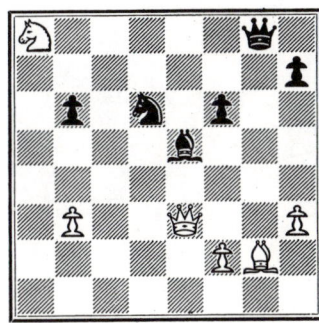

Queen Games

1. Queen against all the Pawns. Can the Black Queen capture all of White's Pawns before one of them queens? White moves first. [A29]

Take turns playing the Queen.

2. Queen against Rook, Knight, and Bishop. White plays first. The winner is the player who captures all the enemy men. Remember that you can have *more* than one Queen if you can queen a Pawn.

This is the most difficult game so far, so do not be down-hearted if you make mistakes at first. It will give you good practice in using all the pieces you have met so far.

The King

The King is the most important man on the board. If he is captured the war is over and the game is lost.

This means that he must be protected at all times. This is made harder because he cannot move fast to get out of danger.

How the King Moves

The King moves, like his Queen, in any direction, but only ONE SQUARE at a time.

It is important to remember that the King can also capture. He can capture an enemy soldier that is standing beside him.

King Practice

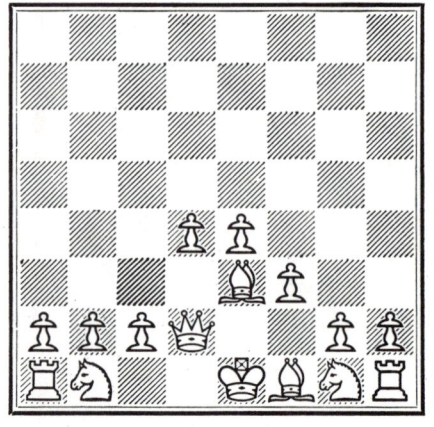

How many squares can the King move to? [A30]

How many squares can the White King move to this time? Can he capture anything? [A31]

ATTENTION!

The King is a very special piece and there are some very special things about him that you need to know. These are so important that they must have sections to themselves.

They are "Check" and "Checkmate".

How many men can the Black King capture? [A32]

Check

When the King can be captured by an enemy soldier he is said to be "in check". The word "check" (and "chess", too) comes from the Persian word *Shah*, meaning "King". The King of Iran is still called the Shah.

When you move a piece so that it threatens your enemy's King, you should warn him that his King is in danger by saying "check". When you say "check" you are really saying "Shah" or "King" or "look out for your King".

When a King is in check one of three things *must* happen:

1. The attacking piece must be captured.
2. One of your own men must move *between* the attacking piece and your King, to protect him. When we do this we "interpose" a man.
3. The King must move out of check.

If you are clever you will see at once that if the attacking piece is a Knight, the second move, as described above, cannot save your King. Can you say why?

Remember a King cannot move *into* check. If he did he would be captured and the game would be over.

Two Kings can never stand next to each other. Why?

Giving Check

Black has just moved his Rook into the corner. There is no piece (Black or White) between the Black Rook and the King. The Black Rook is now attacking the White King. Black says "Check"; White must do something at once. Look at the diagrams.

1. The Bishop can capture the Rook.
2. The White Rook can interpose.
3. The King can move out of check.

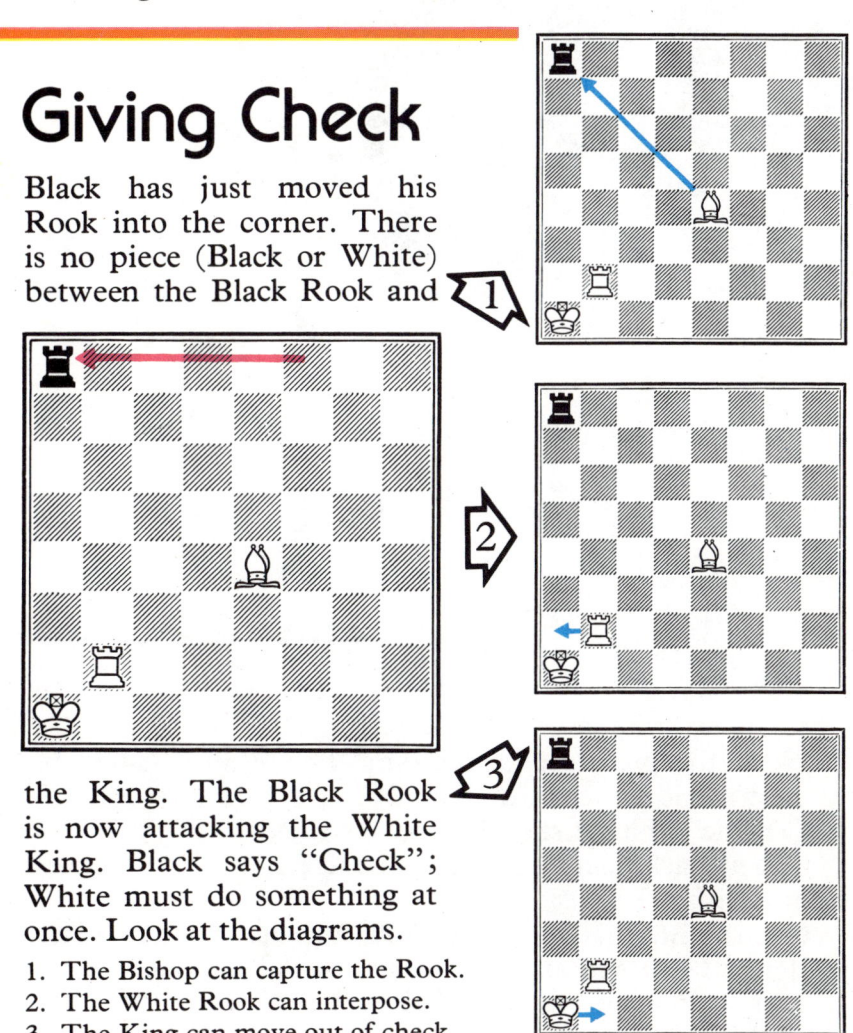

Checkmate

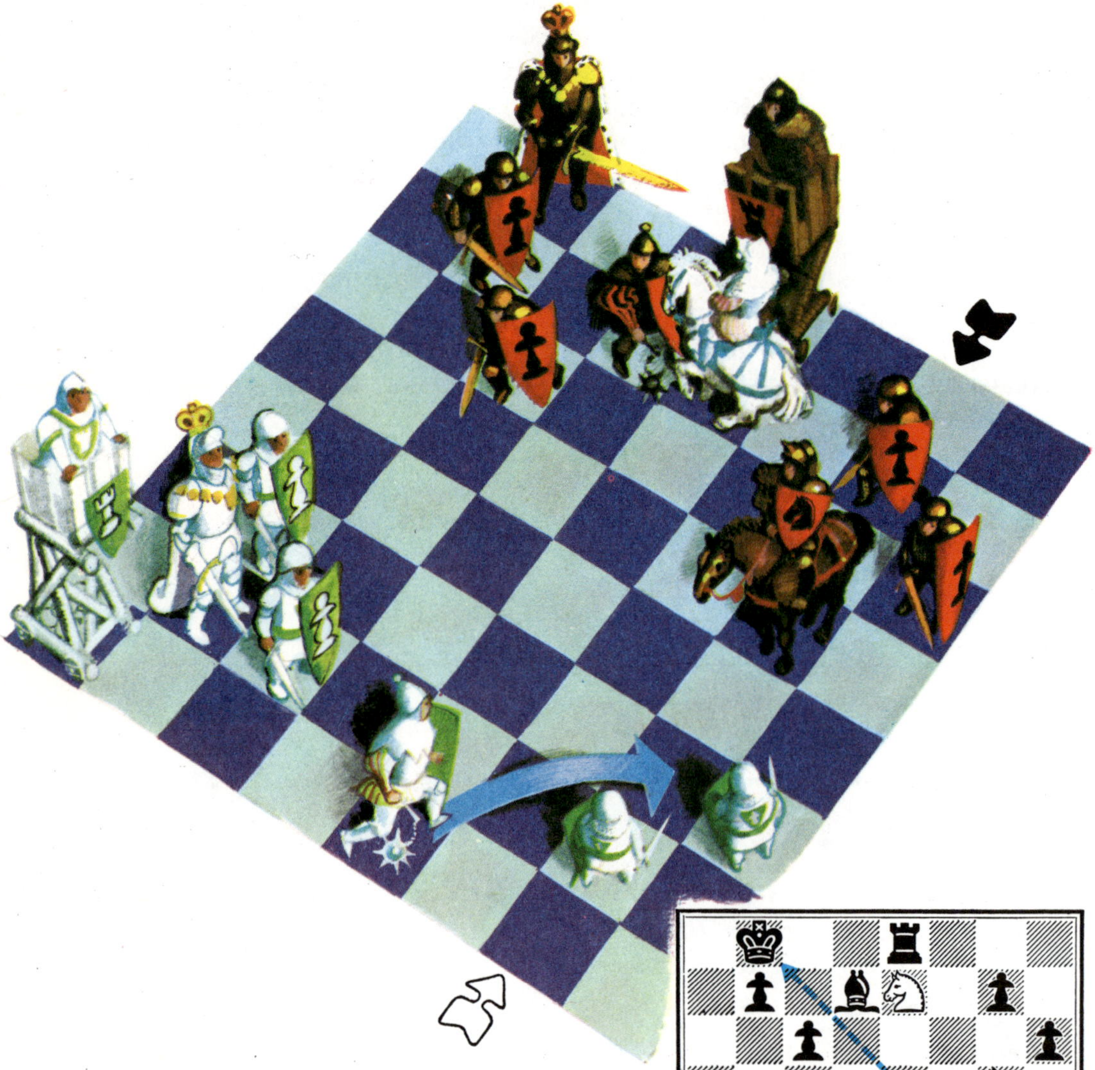

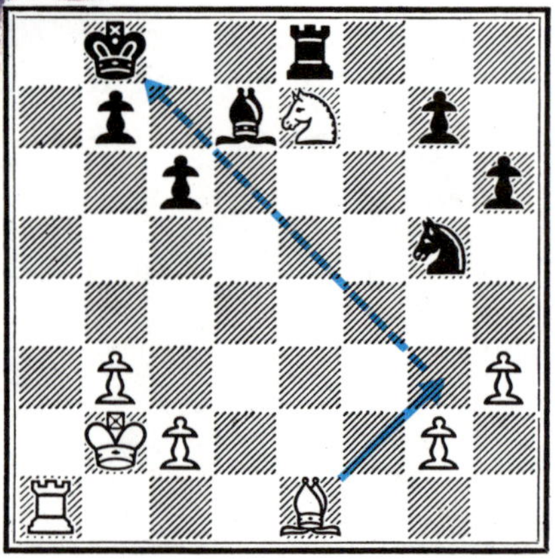

Checkmate Practice is Most Important

In each of these positions White can move once and give checkmate. Can you find the move? If not, set up the board as shown and try again. [*A33, A34, A35*]

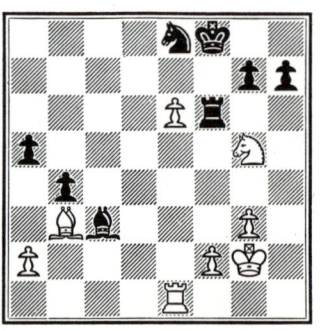

Look at the picture and diagram. The White Bishop moves as shown and attacks the Black King. White says "Check!"

Can the White Bishop be captured? No!

Can a Black man be moved between the Black King and the White Bishop? No!

Can the Black King move without going into check? No!

It is CHECKMATE and White has won. "Checkmate" comes from two Persian words: *Shah mata*, meaning "the King is dead."

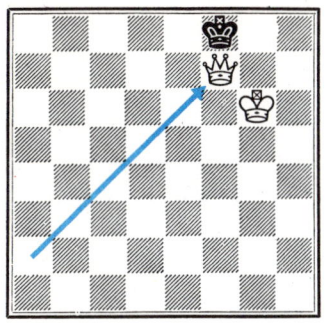

More Checkmates

Here are three different kinds of checkmate. Look very carefully at each diagram in turn and make sure you understand them.
    Notice how in the middle diagram the Black King has been forced to move opposite the White King, which stops him getting away from the side of the board. The Rook can then easily give checkmate.

Now set up the board as shown in each of the two diagrams below and see how many moves you need to give a checkmate similar to those shown in the first two diagrams. Take turns in playing White. (If you play as well as possible you should give checkmate with the Queen in nine moves. Checkmate with the Rook should take you sixteen moves.)

Checkmate Again

1. There is a simple checkmate in one move for White. Can you spot it? [A36]

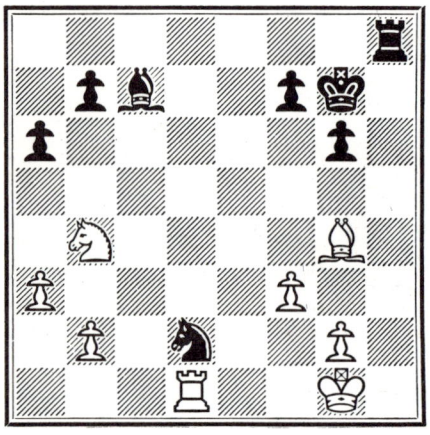

2. This time it is Black to move and checkmate his opponent in one move. [A37]

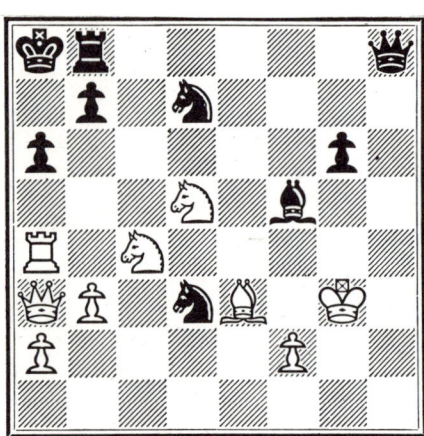

3. White to move and checkmate in one move. If Black moves first he also has a checkmate in one move. Find both mates. [A38]

King Games

1. K + Q against K + R + B.
Set up the board as shown in the diagram. Take it in turns to play White and see if the Bishop and Rook are stronger than the Queen.

The winner is the player who checkmates his enemy. If neither player can get checkmate, the game is a draw. (Remember Pawns can queen!)

Note: If White is left with his Bishop and King against the Black King, he cannot get checkmate and the game is a draw.

2. K + Q + B against K + R + B + N. Now try the game with two extra pieces on the board. See if this makes it easier for one player to checkmate the other.

How many games are drawn and how many end in checkmate?

Attack

Before you can capture an enemy man, you must ATTACK him.

Remember to look around carefully *before you attack*. Make sure of two things:
1. That the square to which you are moving to make the attack is NOT GUARDED.
2. That you do not lose one of your strong men for a weaker enemy man.

Set up the pieces as shown in the picture. The Queen wants to attack the Black Rook. There are *four* squares the Queen can move to in order to do this.

Two of them are DANGER squares. One is a BAD square. Only one is a GOOD square.

DANGER SQUARES: Numbers 2 and 3. Why?
BAD SQUARE: Number 1. Why?
GOOD SQUARE: Number 4. Why?
[See A39]

Attack Practice

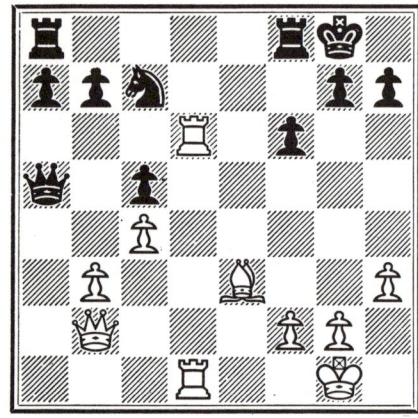

1. It is White to move. He can attack and trap Black's Queen in one move. What is White's move? [A40]

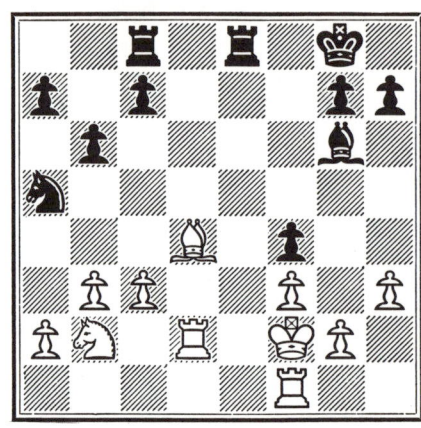

2. Four of Black's men can attack the White Bishop in one move. (a) Which men are they? (b) Which is the best man to use and why? [A41]

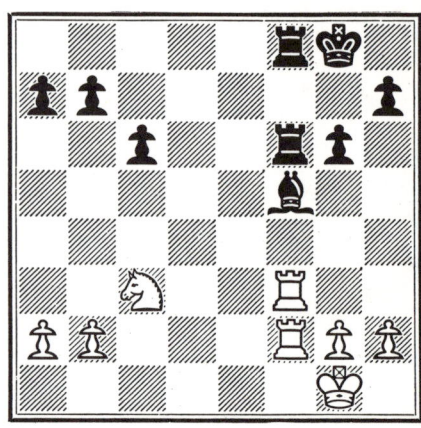

3. It is White to move. A Black Bishop is stopping him attacking and capturing a Black Rook. What can White do about it? [A42]

As we have seen in practice number 3, you do not always mean to capture a piece that you attack. Sometimes you attack an enemy man that is in your way in order to make him move.

When you do this, try to attack with a man of less value than the piece you are attacking – attack a Bishop or Knight with a Pawn, a Rook or Queen with a Bishop or Knight. This is a good thing to remember always, but especially when you want to make an enemy man move away.

Look at the picture. Black can win only if he can queen a Pawn. But both his Pawns are blocked. Can he do something about it?

Yes! He can check the White King with his Knight. This forces the White King to move and frees the Black Pawn.

The Black King then moves as shown. Now White cannot stop Black queening his Pawn in three more moves.

Set up the board and men and try for yourself.

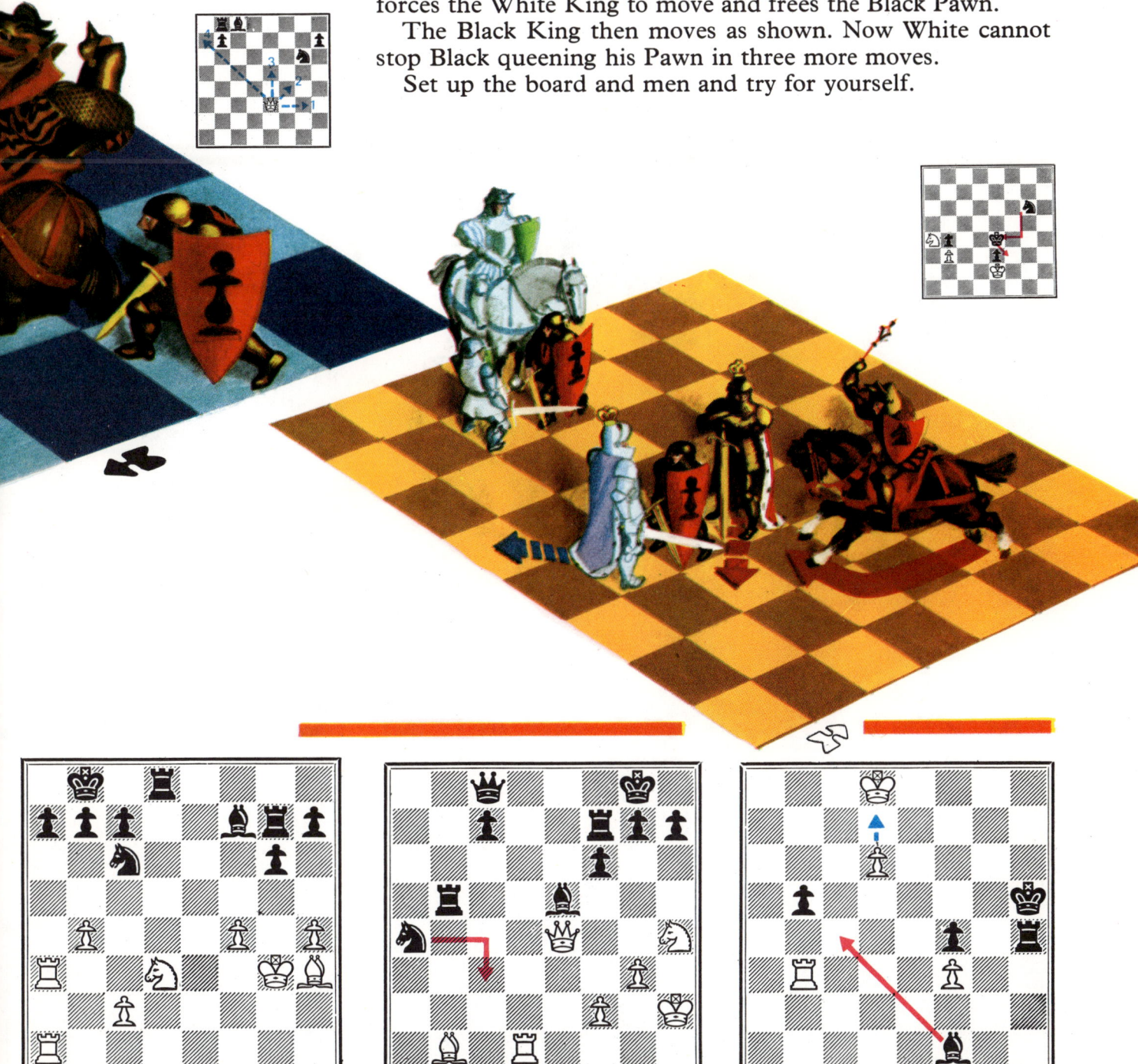

4. White wants to capture the Pawn near Black's King with his Rook and threaten checkmate. How is the Black Knight stopping him? What does White do? [A43]

5. Black's Knight is attacked and he thinks he can make a clever move as shown. He is now attacking White's Queen, Rook and Bishop! What does White do? [A44]

6. Black attacks White's Rook as shown. White ignores his threat and calmly moves forward the Pawn near his King! What should Black do, and why? [A45]

Defence

When one of your men is attacked you can get him out of trouble in the same three ways as you can get your King out of check (see page 29). You can capture the attacking man, you can interpose another of your own men, or you can move the man that is attacked.

But there is a fourth way, when the man under attack is not your King. You can DEFEND the attacked piece. This means you move another man to support the threatened piece so that you can capture the enemy if he takes your piece.

Look at the picture. The Black Rook is attacking the White Rook. White can defend his Rook by moving the Pawn forward to support it, as shown.

Now if the Black Rook captures the White Rook, White can capture the Black Rook with his Pawn. The result is a fair exchange – a Rook for a Rook.

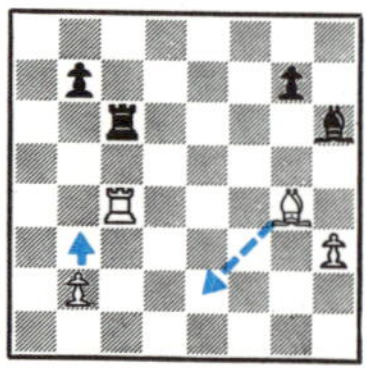

You will see that the White Bishop can also defend the Rook as shown.

Defence Practice

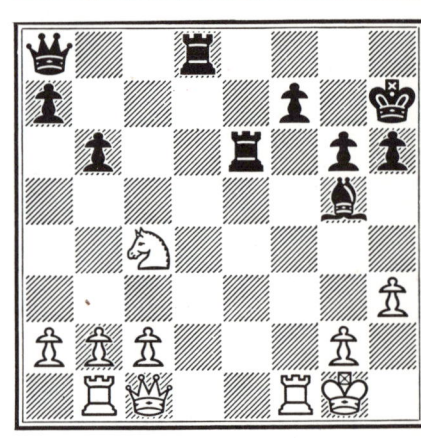

1. White to move. The Black Rook is attacking White's last Pawn. How will White defend it? (A46)

2. Black to move. The White Queen is attacking both Black Rooks at the same time. What is Black to do? [A47]

3. White to move. The White Queen is under attack. How can she defend herself? (*Hint:* attack is the best form of defence!) [A48]

There is one further way yet of getting out of trouble when a piece is attacked. This is to attack a piece yourself. Sometimes attack is the best form of defence.

Look at the first picture. It is Black's turn to move and he moves his Pawn forward to attack White's Bishop. No square to move to! No way of capturing the attacking Pawn! Trapped!

Is there no way out? Yes – attack! White moves his Knight (second picture). Now Black's Queen is attacked. He must make a move to save his most valuable piece. Now White has an escape route for his Bishop, with the Knight out of his way.

So by attacking, White has defended his Bishop successfully.

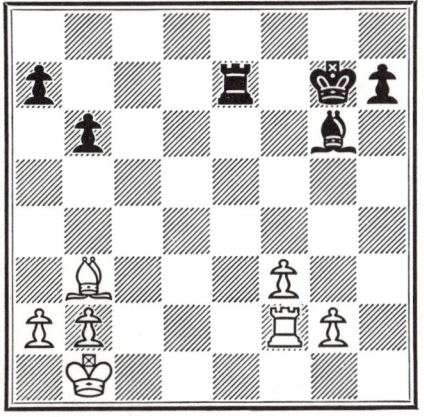

4. White to move. The White King is in check. There are four possible moves for White, but only one can save him from checkmate. Can you find it? [A49]

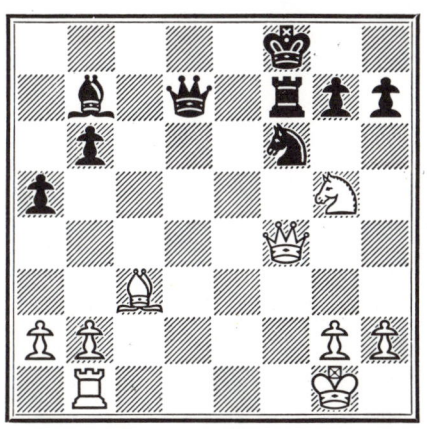

5. Black to move. If Black moves his threatened Rook, the White Knight checks by taking the Pawn on the right with a strong attack. What can Black do? [A50]

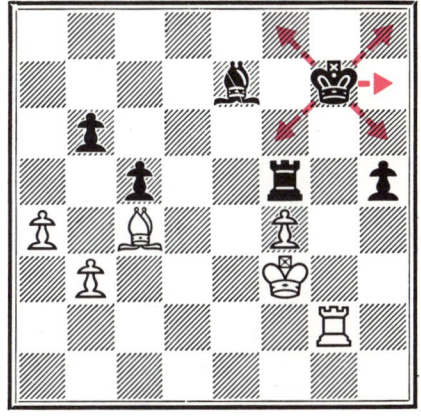

6. The Black King is in check and has five possible moves. One of these gives White checkmate next move. Find which square Black must avoid. [A51]

37

Castling

Before you start an attack on the enemy you must make sure your King is in safety.

There is a special move in chess which helps you to do this. It is called CASTLING. This is because its purpose is to put your king safely in his castle – that is, to use one of your Rooks (or Castles) to protect him.
This is what you do:
1. Move the King *two* squares to his right or his left.
2. Move the Rook that sits on that side of the King to the square next to him *on the other side*.

Look at the pictures and this will be quite clear. Put the King and Rooks on the board and practise until you know these moves well.

So far, so good. But there are other things you have to know about castling. Here they are:
1. You must not have moved the King or Rook before.
2. The squares between the King and the Rook must be *empty*.
3. The King must not be *in Check*.
4. The King must not move through or into Check.

When you "castle", it is the only time you can move two pieces at the same time and the *only* time the King moves more than one square. Of course, you can castle only *once* in a game. It is usually best to castle *on the King's side* of the board.

Castling Practice

Look at these three positions carefully. Can White or Black castle? Set up each position in turn on your board if you want to. [A52, A53, A54]

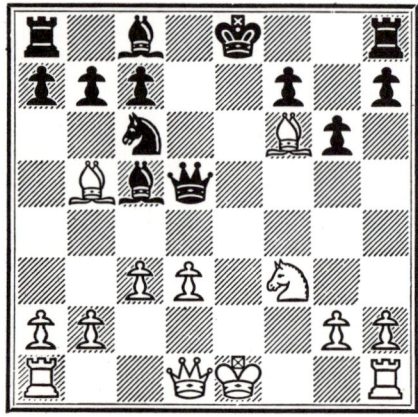
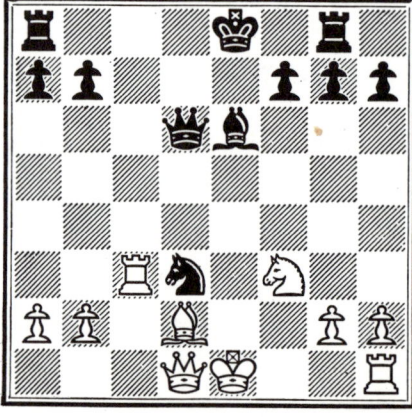
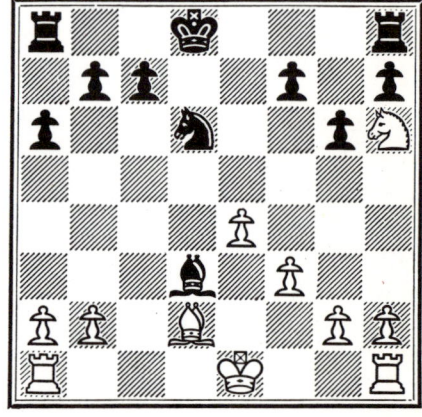

38

The King moves two steps to his right

The Rook moves to the King's left

The King moves two steps to his left

The Rook moves to the King's right

A King's Side Game

Here is a chance to practise all you have learned so far. Set up the board as shown, and play the King's Side Game with a friend. Play it lots of times and take turns to play White, who has the first move.

This game can end in a win or a draw.

A. The game is WON when one player *checkmates* the other.

B. The game is DRAWN when neither player can checkmate the other. This happens when there are only *Kings* left on the board or only *Kings, Knights,* and *Bishops*. Neither side can checkmate the other. Try it and see.

This is real chess, even though you are only using half the men. You have lots of things to remember. Here are some of them:

1. Remember the Pawn's first move.
2. Remember your Pawns can become Queens.
3. Remember, any enemy Pawn can become a Queen!
4. Remember to castle.
5. Remember a Rook is more valuable than a Knight or Bishop.
6. Remember to protect your pieces with Pawns or other pieces whenever you can.

How to Start

1. The first move of all

Set up the board and look at your army. If you need help look back inside the front cover. Remember that all that follows is true whether you are White or Black.

You will soon see that your men are not in the best positions for attack or defence. The Pawns and Knights are the only ones that can move. The King is boxed in and cannot castle. Your first task is to get your men into better positions.

This is called DEVELOPMENT or developing your men. It is the *most important* thing to remember in the opening.

You should move two or three pawns (not more) to make room for pieces, and you should move your Knights and Bishops (and perhaps your Queen) out of the back rank. This will allow you to castle and to move your Rooks along your back rank.

Let us look at each of these in turn.

Moving the King's Pawn frees a Bishop and the Queen

Things to remember

1. Do not move more than two or three Pawns in the opening part of the game.
2. The King needs a protective shield of Pawns after castling. Try not to move any of the three outside Pawns on either side of the board near the beginning of the game, especially the outside three on the King's side.
3. The strength of Pawns lies in their *unity*. Try to keep them supporting each other. Study diagram 1.
4. Use Pawns to protect your pieces.
5. Don't advance Pawns too far too soon. One of them could later become a Queen, if properly looked after.

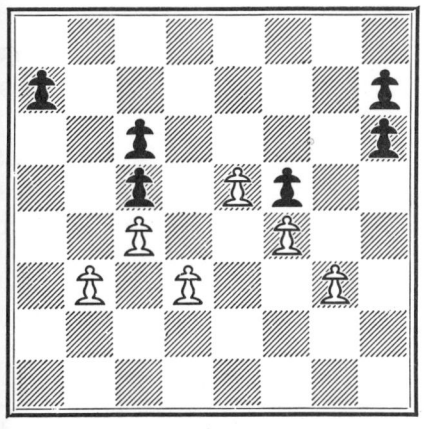

1. White's Pawns are *good*. They are in two compact groups of three. Three of the six Pawns are protected by other Pawns, and the Pawns can protect each other as they move up the board later in the game.

Black's Pawns are *bad*. They are scattered across the board in four *separate* groups. *None* of them is protected by another Pawn. None of them ever *can* be protected by another Pawn. Two sets of Pawns are *doubled* on the same file – this is especially weak.

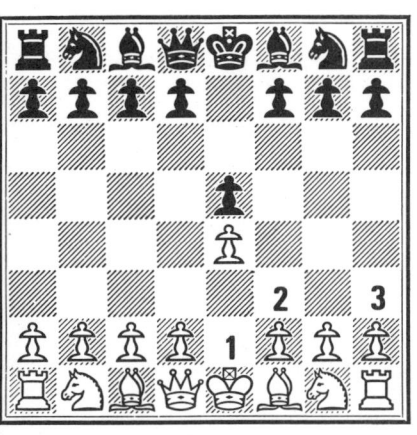

2. Which is the best move for the White King's-side Knight? [A55]

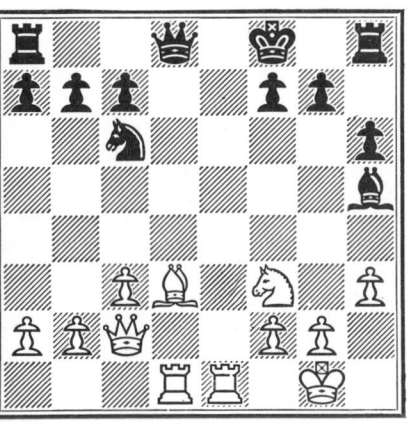

2. Which Pawn to move?

A good first move to choose is one that frees a Bishop to move later on. The two Pawns that are best able to do this are the Queen's Pawn and the King's Pawn. Moving the King's Pawn also opens a diagonal for the Queen. Many players move their King's Pawn two squares for their first move.

3. Knights and Bishops

The *Knight* is a short-range piece, a hand-to-hand fighter. Being able to jump over men, it is especially useful when the narrow no-man's land between the armies becomes crowded. It can also control both light and dark squares. It can be your most valuable piece when other pieces don't have room to move.

Where should it go? There is no absolutely right answer. But if you look back to page 17, you will remind yourself that Knights are more powerful near the centre of the board than they are at the edge. Therefore, if you have a choice, you should *usually* move TOWARD the centre, not away from it. Look at diagram 2.

The *Bishop* is a long-range piece and may not be needed so early in the game as the Knight. But it is a good idea to get at least one Bishop out of the back rank early, so as to allow you to castle. Usually it is better to castle on the King's side, so many players move their King's side Bishop first.

Your Bishops can move safely to any square along the open diagonal, as far as the fifth rank. Remember, however, not to place your Bishops in front of the King or Queen *before* the King's Pawn or Queen's Pawn has moved, or they will be firmly blocked and you will have to waste another Bishop move to free them.

4. Rooks and Queens

These are your heavy artillery and often fire at the enemy from behind the front line. Do not move your Queen into the open too soon, for she can easily be attacked by a humble Pawn, and may have to run for her life.

The Rooks in their far corners are the most difficult pieces to bring into play, so do not be impatient! If you can move your other pieces out of the back rank (not your King, of course), you will be able to move your Rooks to the centre of the back rank, where they will be well placed to control important central files when these are opened up later in the game. Castling helps to bring one of your Rooks to the centre. Look at diagram 3.

3. White's Rooks are beautifully placed in the middle of the back rank. The King's Rook already controls the open King's file, and the Queen's Rook will control the Queen's file and force the Black Queen to move, when White chooses to move his Bishop. (The Black Rooks are still on their starting squares!)

Notice, too, how the White Queen and Bishop are on the same diagonal, like a loaded gun pointing at the heart of the Black King's position.

4. The diagram below shows the position in a game after each player has made six moves. Set up the board and look at the following points.

Black has done everything wrong:

He has moved his Knight with no plan in mind.

His King's Bishop has blocked his Queen's Pawn and so his Queen's Bishop cannot get out.

He has moved his Queen out before his King's Knight.

No Pawn occupies any of the centre squares.

He has not got his King to safety.

He has weakened his shield of King's-side Pawns.

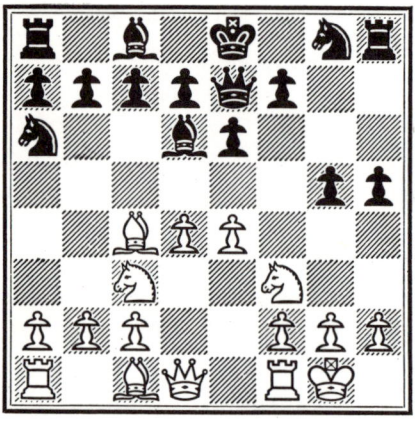

White has done everything right:

He has occupied the centre with Pawns.

His Knights between them cover the four important squares in the centre of the board.

His King's Bishop also fires at the centre and at the Black King's-side position.

He has castled, and so has brought his King to safety, and is ready to move his King's Rook to the middle of the back rank.

His Queen's Bishop is free to move out whenever he wants.

His side Pawns are still intact and strong.

Note: the square in front of your King's Bishop is a danger square. At the start it is protected only by the King and is weak. Watch out for attacks on this square and be ready to take advantage if your opponent doesn't protect his danger square.

More about How to Start

5. A strong centre

The central area of the battlefield is the most important in the early part of any game. The player who controls the centre has supremacy and is well on his way to winning. You can win control of the centre in two ways:

1. Occupy it with Pawns or other pieces.
2. Aim more fire-power at it from a distance than the enemy can.

If you choose the first way, remember to *protect* the Pawns or Knights that you send out on patrol. If you protect them properly, you will at the same time be developing the long-range fire-power needed for the second way. Look at diagram 4 for an example of what to do and what not to do.

6. Picking the best square

Finding the best square to move to is what chess is all about, and good players go on learning all their lives. Luckily, there are a few hints that can help.

1. When you have a free choice, it's usual to move toward the centre or to aim your pieces at the centre.
2. When you have two Pawns that can equally well capture the same enemy man, you should usually choose the one that captures *towards* the centre.
3. Before you move, look carefully at the enemy's last move and try to work out his *next* move. You will then see if there is a threat that you must do something about. Diagram 5 shows what can happen if you don't!
4. NEVER move a man just because you can't think of anything better. Read the next part carefully!

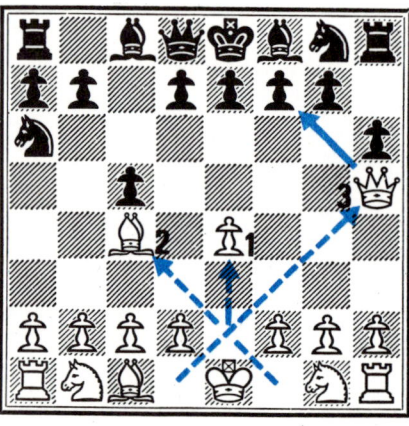

5. An example of what happens when you don't watch what the enemy is up to!

Black has played three bad moves – can you say how they are bad? Even worse, he has played without looking for possible danger from White's moves.

On his fourth move White takes Black's King's Bishop's Pawn and – checkmate!

7. Always have a PLAN!

Always have a plan! This really means: always have a *reason* for the move you choose. Even a bad plan is better than no plan at all. Of course, plans sometimes have to be *changed*. So, be ready to change if your opponent suddenly counter-attacks or makes a move that gives you the chance of a better plan.

Every move you make must have a clear purpose that you can put into words. Ask yourself: "Why am I making this move?" If you cannot give a clear short answer, don't make the move.

Most moves are either *attacking* or *defending* (see pages 34–7) or *developing* (moving a piece to a better square, ready to attack). Be quite clear which you are doing, every time you move.

The last part of this section lists some questions you should keep asking yourself. They will make sure you do make a plan and help you to make a good one. Try to remember them. They are just as important for the middle and end parts of the game. So keep asking them.

8. Ask yourself this:

1. What is my opponent going to do next?
2. Must I defend myself against an attack or can I attack him?
3. *Before I attack*
   - is my King safe?
   - are all my pieces protected?
   - can I easily defend the Pawns in front of my King?
   - do I have open lines to bring up reinforcements or to retreat quickly, if I must?
4. *When I attack*
   - is there an enemy weak spot to attack –
     a Pawn on its own?
     an unprotected piece?
     an exposed King?
   - where should I attack – in the centre, or on the right wing or on the left wing?
5. What is my immediate plan?

Tactics

Once the opening is over, the battle is on in real earnest. It is then that TACTICS come into their own. TACTICS is the name we give to the use of tricks to trap the enemy or lure him into ambush. In this way we wear down his army and make it easier to checkmate him.

Here are some examples.

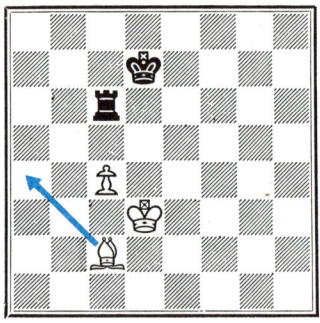
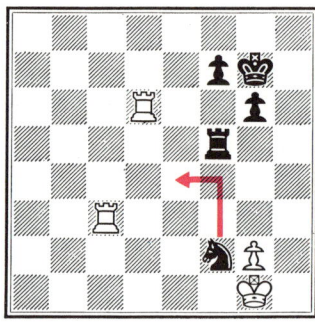

1. White moves his Bishop. Now the Black Rook cannot move, because that would expose his King to check. The Black Rook is PINNED.

2. Black moves his Knight. Now, whatever he does, White must lose one of his Rooks on the next move. The Knight has FORKED the Rooks.

3. White is attacking the Black Queen with his Knight. The Queen cannot escape, so Black captures the Knight with his Bishop, knowing he will lose the Bishop. He has EXCHANGED his Bishop for White's Knight.

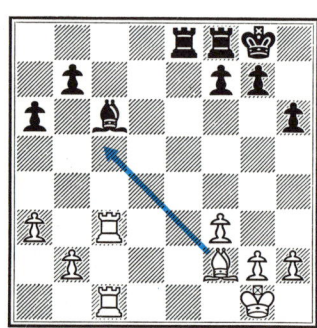
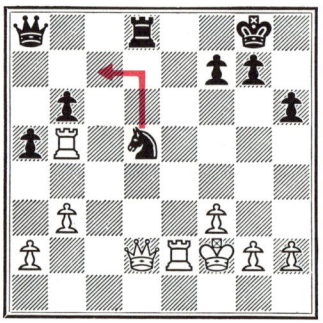
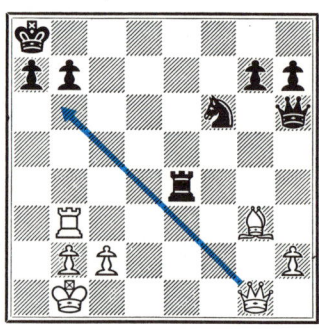

4. White moves his Bishop. Now Black must lose his Rook in exchange for the White Bishop. He has lost the EXCHANGE and White has won it.

5. Black moves his Knight and this uncovers an attack by his Rook on White's Queen. This is called DISCOVERED ATTACK. At the same time the Black Knight attacks one of White's Rooks. White must either lose this Rook, or exchange his Queen for a Rook.

6. White moves his Queen and threatens mate next move. Black can capture it for nothing. But, when he does so, White wins by checkmating Black with his Rook. White has SACRIFICED his Queen.

These tactical tricks are so important that we must look at them more closely.

Pins

When we "pin" an enemy piece we fix him so that he cannot move without leaving a more valuable member of his army open to attack. If the screened piece is the King, the pinned piece cannot move at all. If the screened piece is a Rook or Queen, the pinned piece *can* move, but the Rook or Queen will be lost.

The most important thing about a pin is that the pinned piece is a sitting target for an enemy attack.

Only three pieces can create pins – the Queen, the Rook, and the Bishop. Pins of one kind or another appear in every game of chess. So be on the look-out for chances to use pins and try not to be caught by one. If you are caught in a pin, try to get out of it as quickly as possible.

1. Look at the big picture and set the men on the board. White has foolishly left his King and his Knight on the same dark-squared diagonal.

2. Black takes advantage of this. He moves his Bishop as shown. The unlucky Knight cannot move, because this would leave the King in check from the Black Bishop.

3. White defends the Knight by moving his Pawn one square forward.

4. But, Black attacks the pinned Knight again, with a Pawn. Now the Knight really is lost. Black takes the Knight with his Pawn. A very good capture!

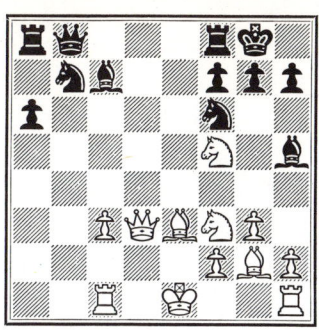

1. If it is White's turn to move, can you find *three* possible pins?

If it is Black's turn to move, can you find *four* possible pins? [A56]

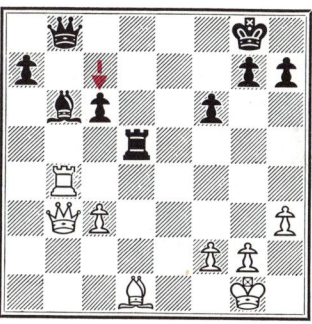

2. It is Black to move. The Black Rook is pinned. Black protects it with a Pawn. Can you find a good move for White? (*Hint*: attack the Rook!)

Can you find two other pins in this position? [A57]

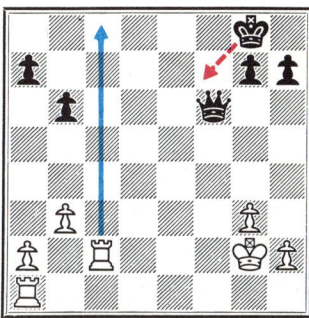

3. *Forcing a pin.* It is White to move. The Black Queen is attacking the White Rook. Instead of moving it away, White makes a much better move, as shown. Check! The Black King must move as shown. What is White's next move? [A58]

Forks

A FORK happens when a man attacks two enemy men at the same time. A fork can be very dangerous. Sometimes it can win a piece for nothing. At best, it makes things difficult for the opponent.

Look at the diagram below. Black moves his Pawn one square forward, attacking the two White pieces at the same time. Only one of them can escape. The Pawn captures the other one on his next move.

REMEMBER to try to work out your enemy's next move before moving yourself.

All your men can fork, even the humble Pawn. But easily the best "forker" is the Knight. It can jump over men. It can be unexpected in the way it moves. Suddenly it seems to spring from nowhere and you find that you are trapped. Watch the enemy Knights like a hawk. Try to see the terrible damage they can do *before* it happens.

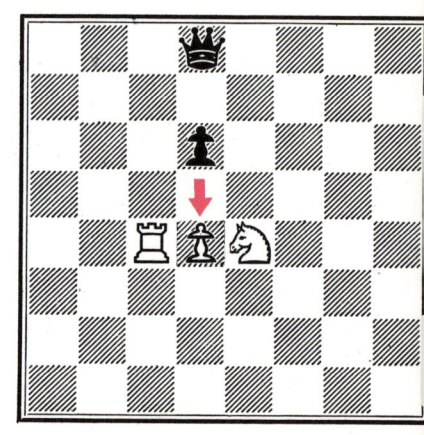

Below is another example. Black was so keen to queen his Pawn that he forgot to check what White was up to. Can you see White's next move?

White moves his Pawn forward. This checks the King AND attacks the Rook. As the White Pawn is protected by the White Rook, the Black King must move. The White Pawn captures the Black Rook next move.

Here are more examples of forks. Study them carefully, for you must learn how to use this powerful trick.

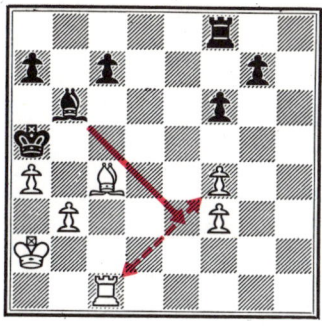

1. *Bishops can fork.* The Black Bishop forks the Rook and Pawn. When the Rook moves out of danger, the Bishop can capture the unprotected Pawn.

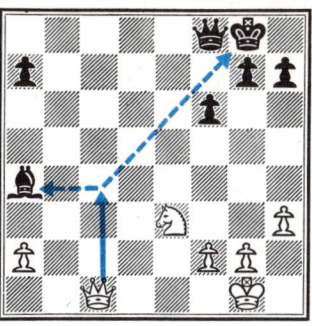

2. *Beware of the Queen!* See what can happen. The Queen moves in one direction, checks the King in another, and attacks the Bishop in yet a third direction. She captures the Bishop on her next move.

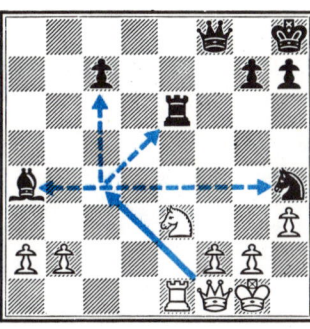

3. *The Queen again.* How powerful and dangerous she is! One moment she is back in headquarters far from the battle. Then in one move she is in the front line attacking four men at once.

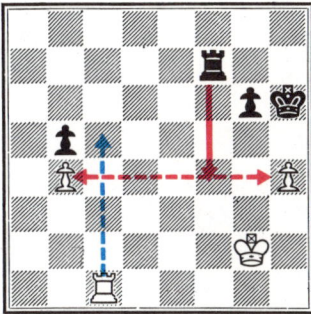

4. *Rooks can fork too.* In the end part of a game, look out for the chance to fork two enemy Pawns with a Rook.

Here White has made it easy for Black, who must now win a Pawn.

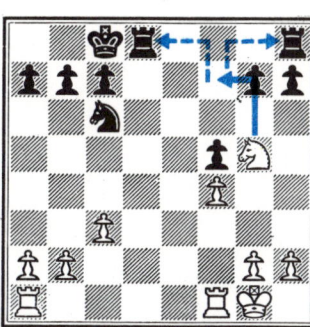

5. *Knight Work.* As a result of castling without looking, Black has left himself open to a simple fork.

The White Knight must capture one of the Black Rooks in exchange for himself.

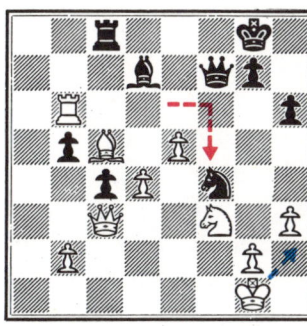

6. *Knights are cunning.* Black moved his Knight as shown. White looked carefully to puzzle out Black's next move. He then moved his King as shown. Why? Was this his best move? [A59]

47

Exchanging

Few games of chess finish without a good number of men of both sides being captured. You must try not to lose men for nothing. So you must try to play so that every time you lose a man you also capture one. When this happens, the players are said to be EXCHANGING men.

What to Exchange

The first thing to remember about exchanging is not to exchange a valuable piece for a less valuable piece. You must learn the VALUE of your men.

You know that the Queen is the strongest piece and the Rook the second strongest. You should only exchange your Queen for your enemy's Queen and one of your Rooks for one of his.

The Knight and the Bishop are very different pieces, but they are about equal in strength. So you can usually exchange a Knight for an enemy Knight OR for an enemy Bishop without any harm being done. And, of course a Bishop for an enemy Bishop OR for an enemy Knight.

Pawns are all equal in value. But remember that Pawns can become Queens, so do not give up *all* your Pawns, even in exchange for enemy Pawns.

A fair exchange. When men of equal value are exchanged – a Pawn for a Pawn, a Knight or Bishop for a Knight or Bishop, a Rook for a Rook or a Queen for a Queen – the exchange is a fair (or equal) one. Neither side has lost or gained anything in strength. Look at diagram 1.

Winning the Exchange. If you can win an enemy Rook for one of your Knights or Bishops you have gained in strength. You have "won the exchange" and your enemy has lost it. Of course, if you can win the enemy Queen for one of your Rooks, that is even better. Remember not to give up *your* Queen for an enemy Rook! Look at diagrams 2 and 3.

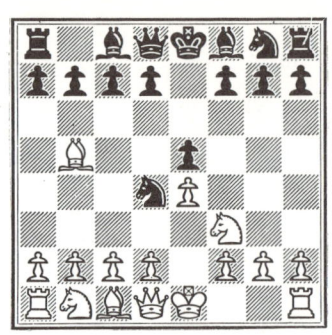

1. White is about to make the first capture of the game. The White Knight captures the Black Knight. Black then captures the White Knight with his Pawn. A Knight for a Knight is a fair exchange.

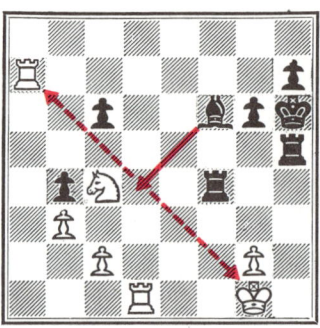

2. The Black Bishop moves as shown. It is now checking the White King *and* attacking a White Rook. The other White Rook must capture the Black Bishop. Black can then take the White Rook with his Rook. White loses a Rook in exchange for a Bishop. He has "lost the exchange".

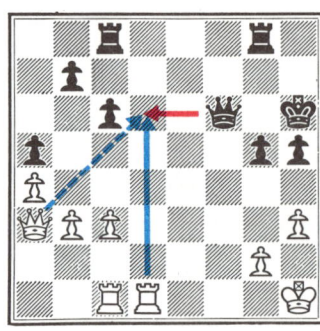

3. The White Rook moves as shown, to attack the Black Queen. The Queen cannot move away, because that would leave her King in check. Black is forced to exchange his precious Queen for a Rook. Don't you fall into this trap.

← Queen for Queen →

> **There are two main reasons for exchanging.**
> 1. *Attacking exchanges.* When an enemy man is in your way, sometimes the only way to get rid of it is to exchange it for one of yours. Look at diagrams 4 and 5.
> 2. *Defensive exchanges.* When you are under attack, sometimes the only way out is to exchange one of your pieces for one of the attacking enemy pieces. Look at diagram 6.

← Rook for Rook →

← Knight for Knight →

← or Knight for Knight →

← Bishop for Bishop →

← or for another Bishop →

← a Pawn for another Pawn →

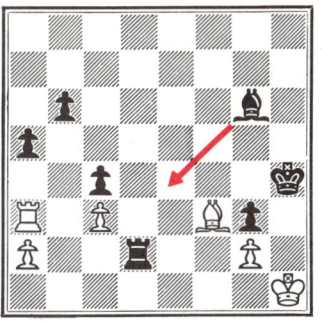

4. Black attacks the White Bishop as shown, because that man is stopping Black from checkmating. If White captures the Bishop the Black Rook will checkmate on the back rank. Whatever White does, Black takes the White Bishop next move. Although White can capture the Black Bishop, Black will soon win.

5. To make sure of queening one of his Pawns, White forces Black to exchange Bishops by moving as shown. Once the Bishops are off the board the Black King cannot prevent White from queening a Pawn.

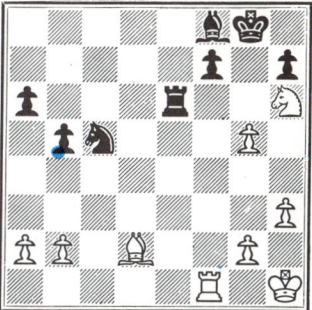

6. The Black King is in check from the enemy Knight, and the Pawn in front of the Black Bishop is threatened. The way out is to capture the Knight. Black can take with either his Rook or his Bishop. Which should he use? [A60]

Discovered Attack

A DISCOVERED ATTACK happens when you move one of your men aside and reveal an attack on an enemy piece from your Bishop, Rook, or Queen. It can be a very nasty surprise, especially if the piece you move aside can be made to attack a *second* enemy piece – two attacks with one move!

In this way you can sometimes win an unprotected enemy piece for nothing. Look back at diagram 5 on page 44. Always remember to protect *your* pieces!

The diagram below shows another simple discovered attack. After Black moves his Pawn as shown, the White Rook cannot escape being taken by the Bishop next move. Black has won the exchange.

If the piece threatened in a discovered attack is the enemy King we call it DISCOVERED CHECK. When the piece that moves aside also attacks the enemy King, we call it DOUBLE CHECK. This is very powerful because it forces the King to move. Look at the diagrams below.

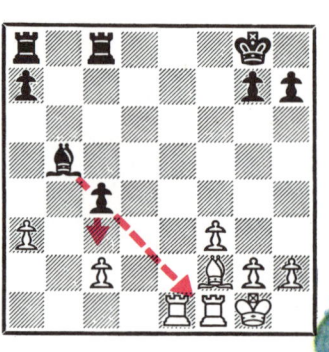

Practice

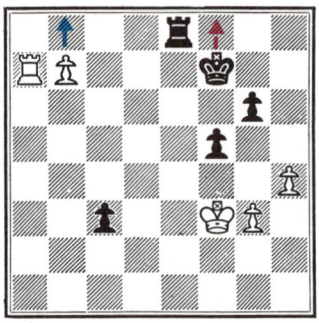

1. White queens his Pawn with discovered check. Because of the check, the new Queen cannot be taken. Now White, with an extra Queen, must win the game.

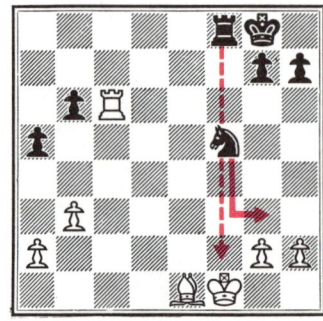

2. Black moves his Knight and gives double check. The King must move. When he does so, it is checkmate next move. Can you see how? [A61]

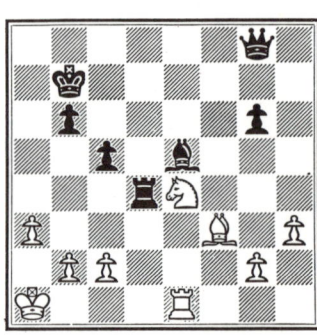

3 White to move. What is the best move? [A62] Set up the board and finish the game with a friend.

Sacrifice

It is all too easy to lose a piece for nothing when you are learning to play. This is a misfortune you try hard to avoid. It is quite different when you give away a piece on purpose, in order to gain some advantage. When you do this you make a SACRIFICE.

Usually, when you offer a sacrifice you are laying a trap. You hope to trick the enemy into thinking he really is getting a piece for nothing. When he takes it you spring an unpleasant surprise on him.

Sometimes the enemy is forced to take the sacrificed piece in order to avoid checkmate, and then you quickly checkmate him in a different way! Look at the first picture for an example.

Sacrifices in chess are exciting to watch and even more exciting to play. Some of them are very clever indeed. But, before you sacrifice, think things out *very* carefully. If you make a mistake you will likely lose the game.

Don't try too hard to find sacrifices. They are quite difficult to see and anyway they don't happen in every game. As you play more and more chess you will begin to see possible moves like this.

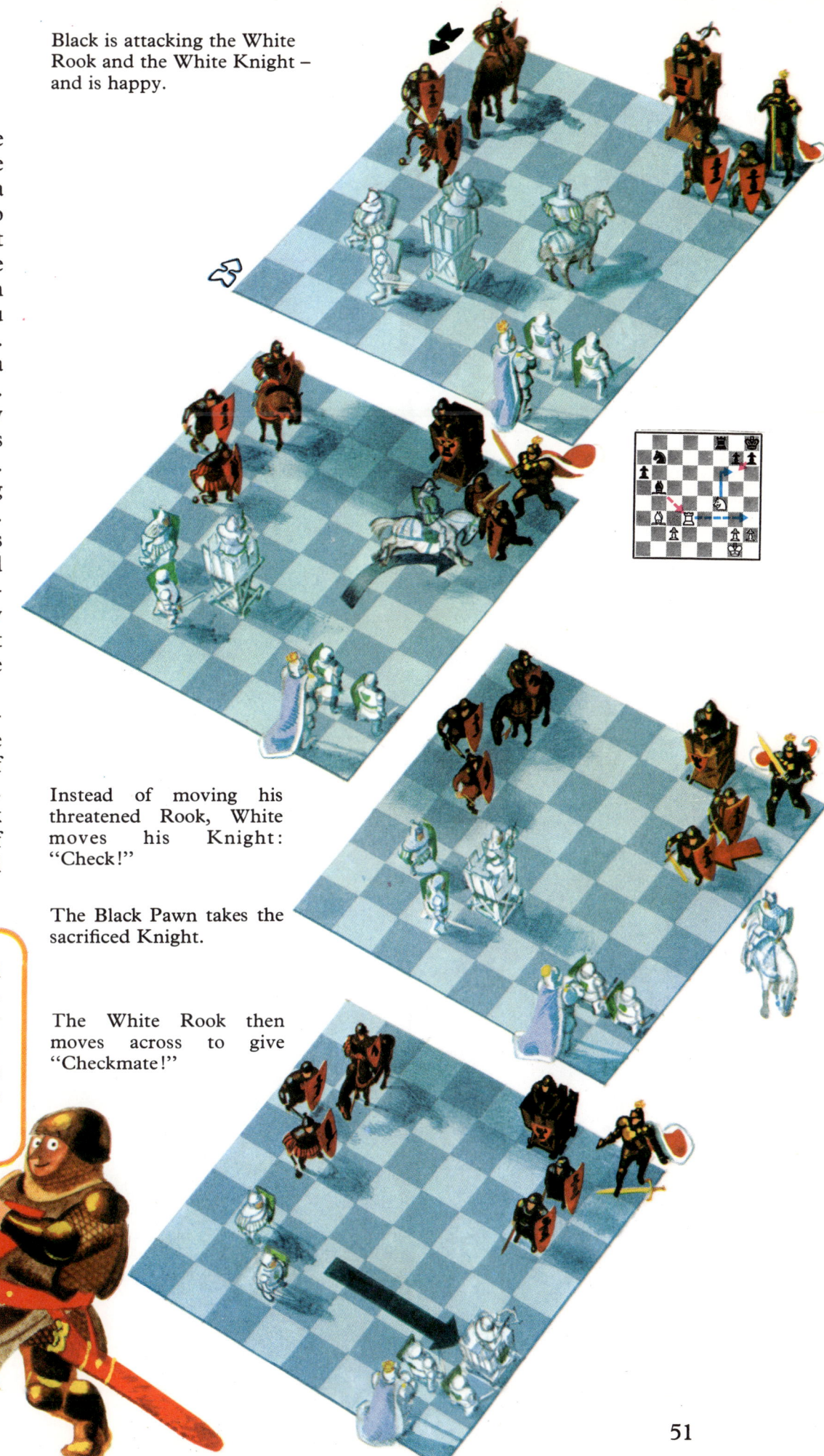

Black is attacking the White Rook and the White Knight – and is happy.

Instead of moving his threatened Rook, White moves his Knight: "Check!"

The Black Pawn takes the sacrificed Knight.

The White Rook then moves across to give "Checkmate!"

51

Sacrifice Practice

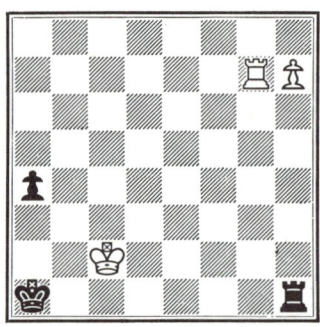

1. White to move. What would you play if you were White? [A63]

2. It is your turn to move and you can choose your colour. Would you choose White or Black? [A64]

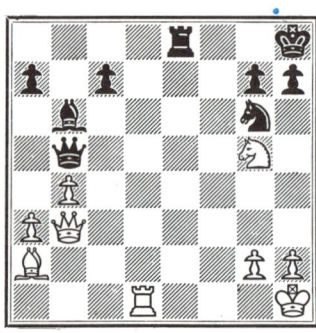

3. White to move. Black's Queen is attacking White's Knight but White is not worried because he has planned a big surprise for Black – mate in two moves! Can you see it? [A65]

How to Finish

1. Without the White King, the Queen could not have given checkmate.

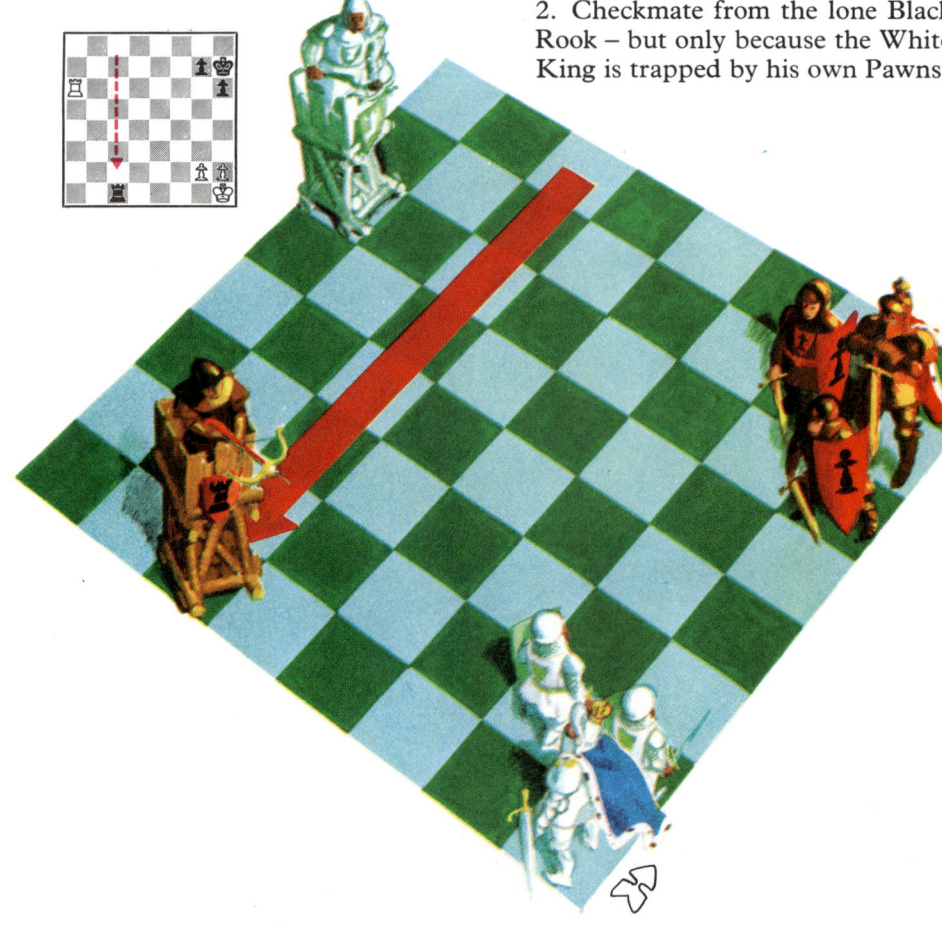

2. Checkmate from the lone Black Rook – but only because the White King is trapped by his own Pawns!

No one piece, not even the mighty Queen, can give checkmate on its own. It takes at least two pieces to force a mate. Look at the first picture. Only because the White King has been brought into the battle is the White Queen able to give checkmate.

It need not be two of your *own* pieces that join forces to produce checkmate. In the second picture it is two enemy Pawns that bring about the downfall of their own King!

In the endgame, when the smoke of battle begins to clear and the two armies have become few in number, the King can venture out of safe hiding. He is no mean fighter either. He can capture enemy pieces and he can stop the advance of an enemy Pawn by placing himself in front of it. Often his help is needed in planning a checkmate. Remember to use your King in the endgame.

The Black King at first has eight squares open to it. After nine moves it has nowhere to go. **Checkmate!**

When you are going after a mate, you must reduce the number of squares the enemy King can move to. In this way, when the final check comes, he will have no square to flee to. Sometimes this takes quite a few moves.

In such cases it is important to make a plan. Look at the ten diagrams (right). See how the number of squares to which the Black King can move is slowly but surely reduced. Notice especially how the White pieces help one another – real team work!

On page 31 you have seen how a King and a Queen or a King and a Rook can check‑

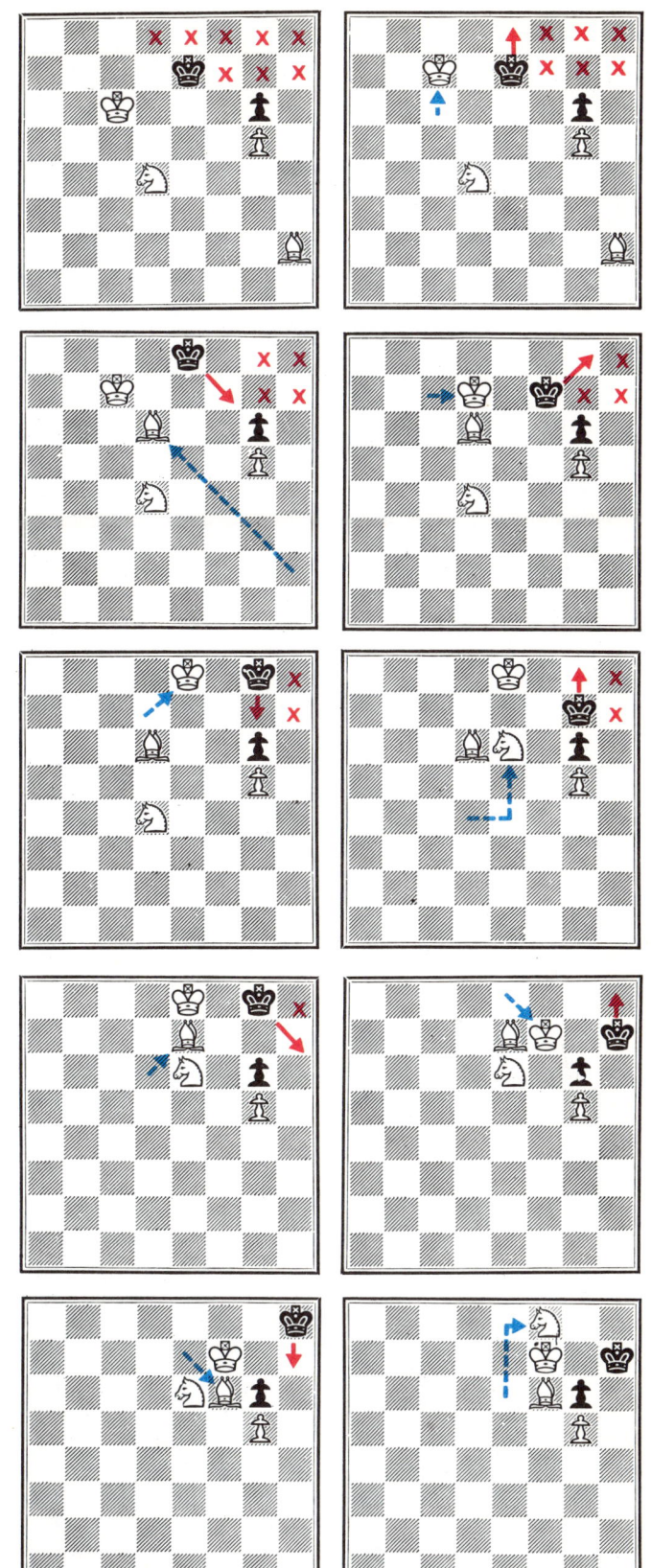

mate a lone King. Look carefully at the final positions in each case until you are sure you have memorized them. When you have done this, you will know what position to aim at.

3. The White King cannot stop the Black Pawn from queening. The Black King keeps him off.

More about How to Finish

But what happens when you have your King and a Pawn against a lone King? You can win, *if* you can get your King *between* your Pawn and the enemy King. Look at the picture above.

BUT notice that if the enemy King is on the same file as your Pawn and ahead of it, the rule is:

1. Your Pawn must not be on either Rook's file.
2. You must get your King in front of your Pawn and one square ahead of it.

Look carefully at diagram 4.

4. **A.** White must win, no matter who moves first. White moves his Pawn one square forward. The Black King must move to one side, allowing the White King to move forward on the *other* side. Now Black cannot stop the White Pawn from queening.

B. A draw, no matter who moves first. The White King cannot advance when the Black King moves aside, and White cannot queen his Pawn.

5. A draw, no matter who moves first. Try it and see for yourself. Find Black's move.

Useful Hints

PAWNS

1. *Take care of your Pawns.* They will serve you well if you do. They are the least valuable of your men, but if you let them be captured for nothing you could be in trouble. They are your first defence against enemy attack. The Pawns in front of your castled King are especially precious.
2. *Do not advance your Pawns too rashly.* This is part of looking after them. Remember *they* cannot retreat and once they are out in front, they are exposed to attack. NEVER advance a Pawn just because you can't think of a better move.
3. *Keep your Pawns together.* Pawns supporting each other are strong. Pawns alone are weak. Try not to have *isolated* or *doubled* Pawns. (See page 41.)
4. *Protect your passed Pawns.* They could become Queens. A passed Pawn is one that has no enemy Pawn in front of it on its own file or on either of the next-door files. Protect a passed Pawn from behind with a Rook on the same file.

DEVELOPMENT

5. *Aim for a strong centre.* You can either try to occupy the centre of the board with Pawns and other pieces or you can direct the fire-power of Knights, Bishops, and Rooks at the centre from a distance.
6. *Bring out your Knights and Bishops.* Get your Knights and Bishops into action as soon as possible after your opening moves and *before* your Rooks and Queen.
7. *Open up paths for your Bishops and Rooks.* Remember these are long-range pieces and need *open* lines to control as many squares as possible. Try not to block your Bishops and Rooks with your own Pawns.
8. *Doubled Rooks are strong.* Look out for a chance to place both your Rooks on the *same* file or rank, so that they support each other. This way they are more than twice as strong.
9. *Support your pieces.* Don't send your men into action without backing them up. Try to put your pieces on squares protected by your Pawns.

PLANNING

10. *Watch the enemy.* Try to work out what your enemy is planning. If you can see what his next move is going to be, decide whether you can ignore it and go on with your own plan, or whether you have to put off your plan and do something about it.
11. *Protect your King.* Try not to leave your King open to attack. If possible, try to keep a protective shield of Pawns or pieces between your King and the enemy army. Don't leave him stranded in the middle of the back rank.
12. *Don't exchange without a reason.* Don't be in a hurry to exchange pieces. It can lessen your chances of winning. Read again pages 48–9.
13. *Watch for a chance to make a passed Pawn.* A passed Pawn is on its way to becoming a Queen. If you get one, you may force the enemy to break off his attack or even to give up a piece in order to capture it.
14. *Always have a plan.* Every move must attack or defend or prepare. Look again at page 43.

FINISHING

15. *Don't fall for a back rank mate.* The game can come to a sudden end if you allow your King to be trapped behind your own Pawns or pieces – see the example on page 52. Never leave your King for long without an escape square.
16. *Use your King.* In the endgame the King comes into his own, in both attack and defence. Its help is especially needed to escort a Pawn to its queening square.
17. *Make sure all your pieces can be used.* Don't let your Bishops and Rooks be shut in behind other men. You *must* be able to get all your men into battle.
18. *Keep out of the way of the enemy Bishop.* If your enemy has a single Bishop in the endgame, try to keep your King, Pawns, and important pieces like a Rook on squares of the *opposite* colour to the Bishop. Then at least one enemy piece can't attack them.

Notation

Chess games can be written down in a kind of code. This is called NOTATION. There is more than one form of Notation, but the one we shall explain is called the Descriptive Notation. This system is used in most chess books at the present time. It is quite simple to learn. The three important things to know are:
1. The *piece* you are moving.
2. The *file* to which you are moving the piece.
3. The *rank number* of the square to which you are moving.

The pieces are abbreviated to a single letter as follows:

        Pawn = P   Rook = R
        Knight = N (or Kt)   Queen = Q
        Bishop = B   King = K

The files are named after the pieces on the back rank. Look at the diagram.
The ranks are numbered 1–8 *from White's side* for White's moves, and numbered 1–8 *from Black's side* for Black's moves (see diagram).

Other symbols you need to know are:

— = moves to
× = takes (captures)
ch = check
0—0 = castles (King's side)
0—0—0 = castles (Queen's side)
e.p. = en passant

Here is a complete game. See if you can play it over on your own board. To help you the first four moves for each player are explained.

      White   *Black*
  1 P—K4   P—K4

White's Pawn moves to White King's 4th rank.
Black's Pawn moves to Black King's 4th rank.

  2 N—KB3   N—QB3

White's Knight moves to White King's Bishop's 3rd rank.
Black's Knight moves to Black Queen's Bishop's 3rd rank.

  3 B—B4   B—B4

White's Bishop moves to White Bishop's 4th rank. (N.B. It is only necessary to say *Q*B4 when the other Bishop can move to *K*B4.)
Black's Bishop moves to Black Bishop's 4th rank.

  4 P—B3   Q—K2

White's Pawn moves to White Bishop's 3rd rank.
Black's Queen moves to Black King's 2nd rank.

If you have played these moves correctly your board should look like this:

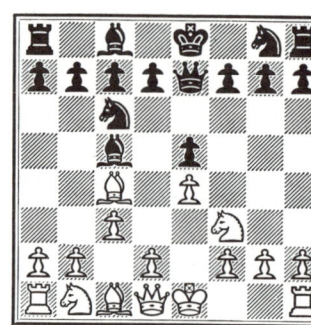

The game continues:

  5 0—0   P—Q3
  6 P—Q4   B—N3
  7 B—KN5   P—B3
  8 B—R4   P—N4
  9 N × NP   P × N
10 Q—R5ch   K—Q2
11 B × P   Q—N2
12 B—K6ch   K × B
13 Q—K8ch   KN—K2
14 P—Q5 mate

Your board should now look like this:

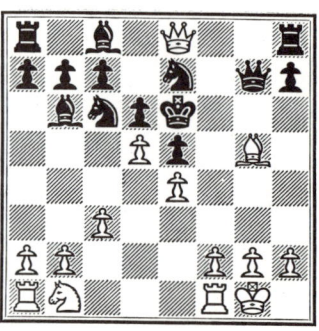

Drawn Games

When neither player can checkmate the other, the game is a draw. The commonest ways in which games are drawn are as follows:

1. *Both players too weak.* It is all too easy to exchange so many pieces that you are left with too small an army to checkmate the enemy King. For example, if the two Kings are left on the board by themselves, neither can checkmate the other, and the game is drawn.

If there are no Pawns on the board, it is impossible to mate the enemy King with your King and a Bishop, or your King and a Knight, or even two Knights.

Therefore, do not weaken your army too much, and try always to keep some of your Pawns on the board.

2. *Stalemate.* If either player, not in check, cannot make any move without moving *into* check, the game is drawn. We call this *stalemate*. Look at diagram 1.

If you have the stronger army and are going after checkmate or planning to queen a Pawn, be on your guard against letting stalemate rob you of victory. Sometimes, a player who is losing can trick his opponent into giving him a draw by stalemate. Look at diagram 2.

3. *Perpetual check.* Sometimes, a player who is losing can get into a position in which he can go on checking his opponent's King for ever. If he can do this, he can claim a draw. Look at diagram 3.

4. *Agreement.* Sometimes, after the game has been going on for some time, both players are left with an equal position, in which neither can gain the advantage. Then one of the players can "offer a draw", and, if his opponent agrees, the game is drawn.

---

1. The White Queen has checked the Black King on the back rank and the King had to move as shown. Now White, in his eagerness to checkmate Black with his Queen in the King's Rook's corner, moves his Knight to cover that square. Disaster! Black now cannot move at all, and the result is stalemate. White has lost his win! Most stalemates happen like this, because the attacking player is too eager.

2. White had an easy win, if he had not moved his Rook's Pawn in his eagerness to queen it. Black is clever enough to see that only his Queen can move. So what is his plan? Get rid of his Queen at once!

Black moves his Queen to KR7 – check. White is forced to capture the Queen with his King. Now Black cannot move. He has tricked White into allowing him stalemate and a draw.

3. White was all set to checkmate Black next move (how?), but Black moved his Queen to the King's Rook file – check. White moves his King to the only possible square. The Black Queen moves to White's back rank – check. The King must move back again. The Black Queen moves back, too – check again. White is helpless. He cannot stop the perpetual check. The game is drawn.

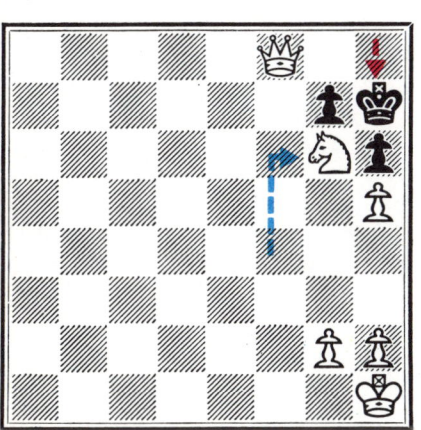
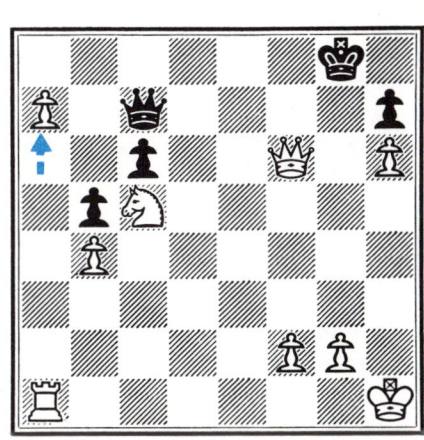
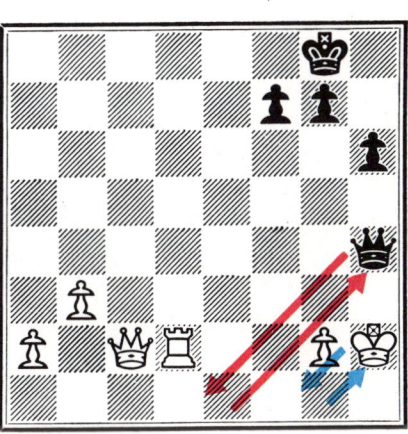

Words You Should Know

You have learned quite a number of special words as you have worked your way through this book. Here are some more words you should know.

En Passant
A French chess term which means "in passing" (say *ong passong*). It is used to describe a special Pawn capture. A Pawn is allowed to move *two* squares on its first move, so that the armies can get to grips quickly.

1. The White Pawn has moved two squares and can be captured en passant.

2. The White Pawn has been captured.

But this is a *privilege* and a Pawn cannot take advantage of it to escape capture.

The rule is: if a Pawn could be captured by an enemy Pawn after moving only *one* square forward, he can still be captured by that Pawn, even if he moves *two* squares forward. Look at the diagrams. Note: the enemy Pawn must make the *en passant* capture at once, on the very next move, or not at all.

J'adoube
Another French term, meaning "I adjust" (say *zhadoob*). Chess players say this if they want to move a man very slightly to put it properly on its square. It is a warning to the opponent that the man is NOT being moved to another square. The reason for the warning is that there is a rule in chess which says that, if you touch a man, you must make a move with that man – *unless* you have said "j'adoube" or "I adjust".

En prise
Another French term, meaning "threatened with capture" (say *ong preez*). A man is *en prise* if it can be captured by an enemy man next move.

Open file
An open file is one on which there are NO Pawns. Rooks like open files. See page 24.

Half-open file
A half-open file is one on which there is only *one* Pawn, either one of yours or one of the enemy's.

Forced move
A forced move is one that the player has to make to avoid being checkmated or to avoid losing a piece for nothing.

Illegal move
An illegal move is one which is forbidden by the rules of chess, like moving the King two squares when it should be moved only one, or moving a Knight wrongly, or leaving a King in check. If a player makes an illegal move, the rule is that he must take it back and then make a proper move *with the same man*, if this is possible.

"I resign"
When a player realises that his position is hopeless and that he must lose the game, it is good manners to give up rather than play on to the bitter end. He does this by laying his King on its side or saying "I resign".

Answers

A1 Danger squares for the Black men are marked with crosses. See diagram below.

A2 The White Pawn on the right and the Black Pawn on the far right are the only Pawns which are not stuck, because either one can capture the other.

A3 A Knight at the side of the board is in control of fewer squares than one in the centre. If a Knight is foolish enough to land in any one of the four corners, he can attack only two squares!

A4 Yes; the Black Pawn on the right.

A5 Yes; the two White Pawns on White's third rank.

A6 The White Knight is attacking four Black Pawns, but can capture only one of them without being captured himself, namely the Pawn on the left.

A7 The Black Knight can move to seven different squares as shown in the diagram below, but six of them are 'minefield' squares, because they are under attack from a White Pawn or a White Knight. The only escape square for the Black Knight is arrowed. See diagram below.

A8 Three Pawns can be captured by the Knight. In each case the Knight's two moves are shown. See diagram below.

A9 Three moves. An interesting thing is that the Knight can capture the Black Pawn in three moves in ten different ways. Can you find them? No wonder the Knight is one of the most cunning men in the army.

A10 No; the Pawn is caught on the Knight's third move. See diagram on page 60. The Knight has a choice of several routes. Two of these are shown.

A11 Yes; quite easily. The idea is to get the Knight on the same file as one of the Pawns and in front of it. In this way it stops the advance of that Pawn. The other Pawn, when it is forced to move forward, is soon captured and the second Pawn cannot be saved. There are different ways of doing this, depending on what moves Black makes. One way is shown on the diagram on page 60.

A12 No; the Pawns are too far apart. If the Knight captures one Pawn it is quite impossible for him to get back to the other side of the board in time to stop the second Pawn from queening.

A13 Eight squares.

A14 The Bishop is attacking the two Pawns on the left side of the diagram.

A15 Black, because the Black Bishop can immediately capture the White Knight for nothing.

A16 Yes. Unlike the Knight, the Bishop is a long-ranging fighter, and can quickly cross from one side of the board to the other. The diagram on page 60 shows the ideal square for the Bishop to be on, with Black to move. Whichever Pawn moves, the Bishop will capture it. Then he will move to a diagonal which the other unhappy Pawn has to cross and that Pawn will be caught also.

A17 Yes; in a similar way to A16.

A18 Ten squares.

A19 Five squares. The Rook can move two squares to its right, two squares straight down the board, *and* it can capture the White Knight!

A20 The Rook is attacking three Pawns – one on the same file as himself and two on the same rank, to his left and right. He can capture the last two without being captured himself. The Pawn on the same file is protected by another White Pawn.

A21 The Black Knight to his left is the only piece the White Rook can safely capture.

A22 White, because White's Rook can move to fourteen squares against the Black Rook's one square. And if the White Rook moves straight down the file to Black's back rank, it stops the Black Rook from moving at all and puts it completely out of the game for the time being.

A23 The Rook can easily capture all four Pawns before one of them can queen because it is a long-ranging piece which can move quickly from one end of the board to the other and from side to side too. The idea is to get the Rook *behind* the Pawns and pick them off one by one.

A24 Yes. If the White Rook moves six squares to the left to protect the Pawn from the front, the Black Rook will move to get behind the Pawn. The Pawn is unable to queen unless the White Rook moves away to another file. Then the Black Rook captures the Pawn. If the White Rook moves down to its starting square in order to protect the Pawn from behind, then the Black Rook moves one square to its right and when the White Rook moves across to the square behind the Pawn, the Black Rook moves straight down the file to block the Pawn. This forces the White Rook away from that file and the Pawn is lost.

It is different if the Pawn is on any other rank (except the 7th). Then the White Rook can get behind the Pawn. No matter what Black does, the Pawn will slowly and surely move forward to the queening square. The Black Rook *can* capture the queened Pawn but will at once be captured himself by the White Rook. On the other hand if it were Black's turn to move first, then *he* would get behind the Pawn, and it would be the White Rook which sooner or later would have to quit the file and leave his Pawn to be snapped up by the Black Rook.

A25 No matter how well Black plays his men, the White Rook is stronger every time. The Black Knight and Pawn cannot for long escape the powerful, long-ranging Rook. The Black Bishop, although wonderfully protected by its Pawn, can control only half the battlefield, but the Rook can

A1

A7

A8

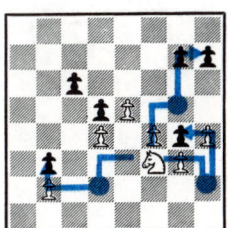

move to any square on the board. Also the White Pawn, protected by the Rook, can march fearlessly up the board to his queening square, knowing that if the Bishop captures him then the Bishop in turn will be captured, leaving the poor Black Pawn at the mercy of the Rook.

A26 Fifteen squares.

A27 If the Black Bishop does not budge, the answer is two moves. But in chess you must always expect the enemy to play the *best* move possible. In that case the answer is three moves. The White Queen swoops up the long white diagonal to the opposite corner square, and attacks the Bishop. The Bishop moves to the only square possible. The Queen then moves along Black's back rank to the white square behind the Bishop. The Bishop cannot escape and is captured next move.

A28 Black. Although the White Queen or White Knight can capture the Black Pawn on the far left for nothing, the Black Queen can capture the White Bishop for nothing. A much better prize!

A29 Yes. The long-ranging Queen can move in so many different directions and is far too strong for the humble Pawns, even eight of them.

A30 The King can move to any one of the three empty squares beside him.

A31 Five. The White King can move to one of the four empty squares beside him. He can also capture the Black Pawn in front of him. (The Black King has two squares to move to.)

A32 Two men, the White Pawn and the White Knight.

A33 The White Queen moves to the black square alongside the Black King – checkmate.

A34 The White Rook moves straight up the file to Black's back rank – checkmate. When a King is caught out like this it is called a 'back rank mate'.

A35 The Black Bishop is attacking the White Rook, but it does not matter to White, because he moves his front Pawn one square forward to checkmate the Black King. The King cannot move to either of the white squares because of the White Bishop. He cannot capture the Pawn because of the White Rook.

A36 The White Queen moves to the white square to the right of the Black King – checkmate.

A37 The Black Bishop moves one diagonal down to the left – checkmate.

A38 White would checkmate by moving his Knight to the square between the Black Pawn and Black Knight. Black would checkmate by moving his Queen straight down to the white square to the right of the White King.

A39 *Danger Squares*. Squares numbered 2 and 3 are both attacked by the Black Knight.
Bad Square. From square number 1 the Queen attacks the Black Rook, but the Rook can escape to the corner.
Good Square. Number 4 is the best square because the Rook cannot escape the Queen's attack.

A40 The White Bishop moves back one diagonal to attack the Black Queen. There is no square for her to escape to.

A41 (a) The Black Knight, the Black Pawn in front of the Black Rook, and either of the Black Rooks.
(b) Black sees two things about the White Bishop. First, it is protected by a Pawn; secondly it has no escape square. Therefore, attack the Bishop with a less valuable man and win a Bishop for a Pawn.

A42 White can attack the Black Bishop by moving the Pawn in front of his King two squares forward. If the Black Bishop refuses to budge, he wins a Bishop for a Pawn. If the Bishop moves away he can capture two Rooks in exchange for one of his own.

A43 The Black Knight is protecting that Pawn. White must try to drive the Black Knight away by attacking it. He moves his left-hand Pawn one square forward. If the Black Knight moves away, then the White Rooks can carry out their threat. If the Black Knight stays put, White will capture it for the loss of a Pawn.

A44 Black's move would usually be very strong, but in this position White was able to start a mating attack. The White Queen, protected by her Bishop, checks the Black King by capturing the Black Pawn at the side of the board. The King must move one square to the left. The White Knight moves forward to check the Black King. Again the King has only the square to the left to move to. Then the White Queen steps on to Black's back rank and deals the decisive blow. When the Black Rook interposes the White Queen captures it – checkmate.

A45 Sometimes an attack fails. This usually happens when a player does not look to see what the enemy can do. It was only when White moved his Pawn one square forward that Black realised the danger he was in. If he takes the White Rook, the White King moves aside, and Black cannot stop the White Pawn queening. All Black can do to save the game is give up his Bishop for the White Pawn by moving along the diagonal to attack it. Had Black looked carefully before he attacked White's Rook with his Bishop, he would have seen that his best play was to get rid of White's danger Pawn. He could do this best by moving his King one square to the left, opening a pathway for his Rook.

A46 The White Rook cannot defend the White Pawn and so it is left to the White King to protect his Pawn by moving one square forward to his left. This puts him on the white square in front of the Black Pawn.

A47 Black must double his Rooks so that they are supporting one another. He can do this either by moving the Rook on his back rank one square to the left or by bringing his other Rook to the back rank.

A48 The only safe way is for the White Rook beside the White King to move up the file, capture the Black Pawn, and give a check at the same time. When the Black King moves, White Queen moves to the white square beside her King, and defends the White Rook which gave the check

A10

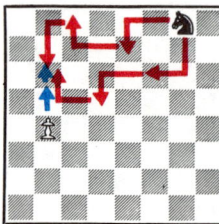

A11

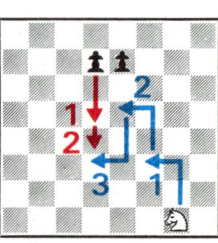

A16

A49 White's four moves are: move King one square to the left or right or interpose his Bishop or his Rook. Black is threatening to move his Rook to White's back rank – checkmate. The only way for White to escape is to move his King one square to the right. Now, if the Black Rook checks on White's back rank, the White King can move out to the black square on his second rank, or White can safely interpose his Bishop.

A50 There is not always a way out. Often one must accept defeat because the other player has played a better game. But in this position there is a way out. Black moves his Queen one square forward to the left. Now Black is threatening mate by the Black Queen capturing the White Pawn in front of the White King. White must prevent the mate and this gives Black a chance to move his Rook out of danger on his next move.

A51 The five squares the Black King can move to are the four black squares beside him and the white square on the right edge of the board. The one square the Black King must avoid is the black square on his back rank near the Black Bishop. If he gets there, the White Rook will swoop up the board to the white square beside him and say "checkmate".

A52 White cannot castle. On the Queen's side the Queen herself is in the way, and on the King's side the Black Bishop is guarding the black square to which the King would have to move. Black cannot castle on the Queen's side because of the Black Bishop, but may castle on the King's side if he wishes. It does not matter that the Rook is attacked by the White Bishop.

A53 White cannot castle because his King is in check from the Black Knight. Black cannot castle. On the Queen's side the White Rook is guarding the white square to which the King would have to move, and on the King's side the Black Rook has already moved.

A54 White can castle on the Queen's side. A Rook *can* cross over a square guarded by the enemy. White cannot castle on the King's side because a King *cannot* cross over a square guarded by the enemy. In this case the Black Bishop is guarding the white square to the right of the White King. Black cannot castle on either side because the Black King has moved!

A55 It is usually best to place the King's Knight on square 2, where it attacks two of the four centre squares. If the King's-side Bishop has moved away from its starting square, the Knight is sometimes moved to the white square in front of the King. This allows the Pawn in front of the Bishop to move one square forward in support of his King's Pawn.

A56 *White.* (1) Move the left-hand Rook one square to the left. It now pins the Black Knight against the Black Queen. (2) This one is not quite so easy to see. Move the Knight nearest to the White King and then the white-squared Bishop is pinning the same Black Knight against the Black Rook. (3) Move the Queen one square forward to the left and she is pinning the Black Pawn against the Black King. This is not a very useful pin at the moment because the Black Pawn cannot move anyway. If the black-squared Bishop moves forward one square to the right, the Black Bishop is not pinned on the Black Queen because it can capture the White Bishop any time it likes.
Black. (1) Move the black-squared Bishop to the left side of the board and it is pinning the White Pawn against the White King. (2) Move the white-squared Bishop one square back and it pins the White Knight against the White Queen. (3) and (4) Move either the Black Rook near the King or the Black Queen to the white square opposite the White King and the White Bishop is pinned against the White King.

A57 A good move for White is to attack the Black Rook again with a lesser piece – the Bishop. Move the White Bishop three squares along the diagonal to the right. On the next move the Black Rook is captured by the Bishop in exchange for itself – a good bargain.
Other pins. The White Pawn on the black square next to his King is pinned by the Black Bishop, and the Black Bishop is itself pinned by the White Rook.

A58 White moves his other Rook five squares along his back rank and pins the Black Queen!

A59 The King moved away because he saw the very real danger of the Black Knight moving to give check, forking the Queen at the same time, and capturing it next move. That was good. But sometimes there is more than one threat. Before making a move you must have one more look to see if there is anything else the enemy is up to. Black's main threat was certainly to fork the White King and Queen with his Knight. But he was also threatening to move his Knight back on to the white square beside the White Bishop to fork the White Queen and Rook. As the White Queen was part of both forks it was the Queen who should have moved, not the White King.

A60 He should take with the Bishop for that will make it a fair exchange – a Knight for a Bishop.

A61 The White King's only move is to the black square on his right, and then the Black Rook comes straight down the board to the square that the King has just left – checkmate. You will notice that the Black Knight was able to land on a minefield square without being captured, because the Black Rook was also checking the White King.

A62 Black has much the stronger army but he has carelessly left his Queen on a bad square. The White Knight moves and discovers a check on Black King from White's Bishop. Black must do something about the check and because the White Knight can move to a square from which it attacks Black's Queen, Black must lose his Queen. Now finish the game.

A63 Bring the White Rook right up beside the Black Rook and give check to the Black King. The Black Rook is forced to capture the White Rook otherwise he himself will be captured. Then the White Pawn can be safely queened and at the same time give check to the Black King. White wins the game next move.

A64 Choose White because there is a beautiful Queen sacrifice that allows White to win the game. The White Queen moves up the long white diagonal to the white corner square beside Black's King – check. The Black King must capture the enemy Queen. Then the White Rook moves straight up the board to Black's back rank – checkmate.

A65 Another Queen sacrifice. The White Queen moves up the diagonal to the white square beside the Black King – check. The Black Rook is forced to take the White Queen and then quite calmly the White Knight moves forward to the white square to the left of the Black Pawn to deal the death blow! This is called a 'smothered' mate.

The position of the men at the start. White has made his first move. Each Queen starts the game on a square of her own colour – the White Queen on a white square, the Black Queen on a black square.